DUCHESSES IN BAVARIA

Table of Contents

Duchess Amalie in Bavaria 1
Duchess Helene in Bavaria 2
Duchess Marie Gabrielle in Bavaria ... 3
Duchess Mathilde Ludovika in
Bavaria 5
Duchess Sophie Charlotte in Bavaria . 5
Dukes in Bavaria 6
Elisabeth of Bavaria, Queen of Belgium 8
Empress Elisabeth of Austria 10
Infanta Maria Josepha of Portugal 19
Maria Sophie of Bavaria 20
Marie of Baden-Sponheim 22
Princess Amalie of Saxe-Coburg and
Gotha 22
Princess Amélie Louise of Arenberg 23
Princess Ludovika of Bavaria 23
Princess Sophie of Saxony 24
Sophie, Hereditary Princess of Liechtenstein 25

Preface

Each chapter in this book ends with a URL to a hyperlinked online version. Use the online version to access related pages, websites, footnotes, tables, color photos, updates, or to see the chapter's contributors. Click the edit link to suggest changes. Please type the URL exactly as it appears. If you change the URL's capitalization, for example, it may not work.

Purchase of this book entitles you to a free trial membership in the publisher's book club at www.booksllc.net. (Time limited offer.) Simply enter the barcode number from the back cover onto the membership form on our home page. The book club entitles you to select from millions of books at no additional charge, including a digital copy of this and related books to read on the go. Simply enter the title or subject onto the search form to find them.

If you have any questions, could you please be so kind as to consult our Frequently Asked Questions page at www. booksllc.net/faqs.cfm? You are also welcome to contact us there.

Publisher: Books LLC, Wiki Series, Memphis, TN, USA, 2012.

Duchess Amalie in Bavaria

Duchess Amalie in Bavaria
Duchess of Urach

Spouse Wilhelm, 2nd Duke of Urach
Issue
Princess Marie Gabriele
Princess Elisabeth
Princess Karola
Prince Wilhelm
Karl Gero, Duke of Urach
Princess Margarete
Prince Albrecht
Prince Eberhard
Princess Mechtilde
Full name
German: *Amalie Maria*
House House of Wittelsbach
House of Württemberg
Father Duke Karl-Theodor in Bavari
Mother Princess Sophie of Saxony
Born 24 December 1865
Munich, Kingdom of Bavaria
Died 26 May 1912 (aged 46)
Stuttgart, Kingdom of Württemberg

Duchess *Amalie* Maria in Bavaria (Full German name: *Amalie Maria, Herzogin in Bayern*) (24 December 1865 – 26 May 1912) was born in Munich, Kingdom of Bavaria, the only child of Duke Karl-Theodor in Bavaria and his first wife Princess Sophie of Saxony. Amalie was a member of the House of Wittelsbach and a Duchess in Bavaria by birth and a member of the House of Württemberg and Duchess of Urach and Countess of Württemberg through her marriage to Wilhelm, 2nd Duke of Urach.

Marriage and issue

Amalie married Wilhelm, 2nd Duke of Urach (later Mindaugas II of Lithuania), eldest son of Wilhelm, 1st Duke of Urach and his second wife Princess Florestine of Monaco, on 4 July 1892 in Tegernsee, Kingdom of Bavaria. Amalie and Wilhelm had nine children:
Princess Marie Gabriele of Urach (1893–1908)
Princess Elisabeth of Urach (1894–1962) who married Prince Karl of Liechtenstein (1878–1955), an uncle of Franz Joseph II of Liechtenstein, and had issue.
Princess Karola of Urach (1896–1980)
Prince Wilhelm of Urach (1897–1957), who morganatically married Elisabeth Theurer (1899–1988) and had two daughters, Elisabeth and Marie Christine, neither of whom married.
Karl Gero, Duke of Urach (1899–1981), 3rd Duke, who married Countess Gabriele of Waldburg of Zeil and Trauchburg (1910–2005). No issue.
Princess Margarete of Urach (1901–1975)
Prince Albrecht of Urach (1903–1969). Married first Rosemary Blackadder and

second Ute Waldschmidt. Divorced both of them and had issue by both. His daughter Marie-Gabrielle (aka Mariga) was the first wife of Desmond Guinness. A diplomat and artist turned journalist and expert on the Far East. His marriages were also considered morganatic but his descendants can claim titles that pass in the eldest female line.

Prince Eberhard of Urach (1907–1969), who married Princess Iniga of Thurn and Taxis (1925–2008) and had issue; including Karl Anselm and Wilhelm Albert the current and 5th Duke of Urach. While a notional pretender to the crown of Lithuania, he has not made a formal public claim. Eberhard's descendants inherit the dukedom on the basis of the Salic law principle of Agnatic primogeniture

Princess Mechtilde of Urach (1912–2001), who married Friedrich Karl, Prince of Hohenlohe-Waldenburg-Schillingsfürst and had issue.

Amalie died at Stuttgart, Kingdom of Württemberg, in 1912, aged 47, following the birth of her ninth child.

Titles, styles, honours and arms

Titles and styles

24 December 1865 – 4 July 1892: *Her Royal Highness* Duchess Amalie in Bavaria

4 July 1892 – 26 May 1912: *Her Royal Highness* The Duchess of Urach, Countess of Württemberg, Duchess in Bavaria

Ancestry

Source http://en.wikipedia.org/wiki/Duchess_Amalie_in_Bavaria

Duchess Helene in Bavaria

Duchess Helene in Bavaria
Hereditary Princess of Thurn and Taxis

Spouse	Maximilian Anton Lamoral, Hereditary Prince of Thurn a Taxis
Issue	

Princess Louise of Hohenzollern
Elisabeth, Duchess of Braganza
Maximilian Maria, 7th Prince of Thurn Taxis
Albert, 8th Prince of Thurn and Taxis

Full name
German: *Caroline Therese Helene*

House	House of Wittelsbach House of Thurn and Taxis
Father	Duke Maximilian Joseph in Bavaria
Mother	Princess Ludovika of Bavaria
Born	4 April 1834 Munich, Kingdom of Bavaria
Died	16 May 1890 (aged 56) Regensburg, Kingdom of Ba
Burial	Gruftkapelle, Saint Emmerar Abbey, Regensburg
Religion	Roman Catholic

Helene Caroline Therese, Duchess in Bavaria (4 April 1834 – 16 May 1890) of the House of Wittelsbach, nicknamed Néné, was a Bavarian princess and, through marriage, temporarily the head of the Thurn and Taxis family.

Family

Helene was the oldest daughter of Maximilian Joseph, Duke in Bavaria and Ludovika, Royal Princess of Bavaria. The family home was at Possenhofen Castle.

Marriage

In 1853 she traveled with her mother Ludovika and her younger sister Elisabeth to the resort of Bad Ischl, Upper Austria with the hopes that she would become the bride of their cousin Franz Josef, then the emperor of Austria. He decided that he preferred Elisabeth instead. Helene was unusually pious, and would have fit into the Habsburg court well. She had one quality, though, that would not have been accepted: she was habitually late, and often missed trains and appointments.

After the failed engagement, she became depressed and Ludovika became concerned that Helene would take the veil and join a convent. Helene had almost come to terms with remaining single. At 22 years old she was considered to be an "old maid," but her mother

Helene's husband Maximilian

arranged for her to meet the wealthy Maximilian Anton Lamoral, Hereditary Prince of Thurn and Taxis. Duke Max in Bavaria, Helene's father, invited the Thurn and Taxis family to Possenhofen for a hunting party, at which Prince Maximilian was introduced to Helene.

While the prince was vacationing at Possenhofen, he brought his marriage plans to his parents, who immediately agreed. The only difficulty involved was that although the Thurn and Taxis family were counted among the richest in the land, they were not considered social equals for a princess of royal blood and a member of the House of Wittelsbach. Because of this, King Maximilian II of Bavaria did not at first agree to a marriage between the two, but through Elisabeth's influence on the king, the marriage took place nevertheless. The wedding ceremony was held on 24 August 1858 at Possenhofen. To mark the occasion, the in-laws gave the bride a necklace worth 160,000 Gulden. Ironically, in spite of the earlier objections to the match, Helene is considered to have had the only happy marriage among the five Wittelsbach sisters.

Her daughter Louisa was born in 1859, followed by a second daughter, Elisabeth, in 1860. Shortly after the birth of her second child she traveled to Corfu to visit her sister Elisabeth, who was very ill. She returned by way of Vienna, where she reported to Franz Josef on the poor state of his wife.

She gave birth to the much-desired son in 1862, named Maximilian Maria, and in 1867 had another son named Albert.

Even though the couple had a happy marriage, it was overshadowed by the severe illness of her husband Maximilian, who had chronic kidney disease. Neither a course of treatment in Karlsbad nor the best doctors could save him. He died in 1867 at only 36 years of age.

Later life

Helene took her mind off her sorrows with charitable activities. She received the guardianship of her children from the Austrian emperor. Her father-in-law began to include her in the business affairs of the House of Thurn and Taxis, seeing in her a support and successor. In this way she became the head of the family until her oldest son reached his majority.

In 1877 her youngest daughter Elisabeth married Prince Miguel of Braganza, the Miguelist claimant to the throne of Portugal. Elisabeth's health deteriorated after the birth of her first child, and she eventually died in 1881.

In 1879 Helene's oldest daughter Louise married the young Prince Frederick of Hohenzollern-Sigmaringen. The couple had no children.

In 1883, her son Maximilian took over the leadership of the family business, but the well-trained young man fell ill. His heart had been weakened by scarlet fever in childhood, and he suffered from severe heart spasms. In 1885, he died of a pulmonary embolism. This left Helene the family head again, until 1888 when her son Albert reached his majority and took over the family businesses. Helene then retired and dedicated herself to her religious devotions.

She became very ill with stomach cancer in 1890, and her sister Elisabeth hurried to her side. Elisabeth was the last person to speak with Helene. Elisabeth's daughter Marie Valerie related in her diary, "Aunt Néné ... was glad to see Mama and said to her, 'Old Sisi' -- she and Mama almost always spoke English together. 'We two have had hard puffs in our lives,' said Mama. 'Yes, but we had hearts,' replied Aunt Néné."

Titles, styles, honours and arms

**Styles of
Helene, Hereditary Princess of Thurn and Taxis**

Reference style	Her Royal Highness
Spoken style	Your Royal Highness
Alternative style	Ma'am

Titles and styles

4 April 1834 – 24 August 1858 *Her Royal Highness* Duchess Helene in Bavaria

24 August 1858 – 16 May 1890 *Her Royal Highness* the Hereditary Princess of Thurn and Taxis

Ancestry

Source   http://en.wikipedia.org/wiki/Duchess_Helene_in_Bavaria

Duchess Marie Gabrielle in Bavaria

Marie Gabrielle of Bavaria
Princess Rupprecht of Bavaria

Duchess Marie Gabrielle in Bavaria

Duchess Marie Gabrielle in Bavaria, photograph taken circa 1900

Spouse Rupprecht, Crown Prince of Bavaria

Issue
Prince Luitpold of Bavaria
Princess Irmingard of Bavaria
Albrecht, Duke of Bavaria
Prince Rudolf of Bavaria

Full name
German: *Marie Gabrielle Mathilde Isabelle Therese Antoinette Sabine Herzogin in Bayern*

House	House of Wittelsbach
Father	Duke Karl-Theodor in Bavaria
Mother	Infanta Maria Josepha of Portugal
Born	9 October 1878 Tegernsee, Bavaria
Died	24 October 1912 (aged 34) Sorrento, Italy

Duchess Marie Gabrielle in Bavaria (German: *Marie Gabrielle Mathilde Isabelle Therese Antoinette Sabine Herzogin in Bayern*; October 9, 1878 in Tegernsee, Bavaria – October 24, 1912 in Sorrento, Italy).

Biography

Family

Her parents were Duke Karl-Theodor in Bavaria, kinsman to the Kings of Bavaria and world renowned ophthalmologist, and his second wife, Princess Maria José of Bragança, a daughter of King Miguel I, exiled monarch of Portugal. Her paternal aunt was Empress Elisabeth of Austria (*Sissi*) and one of her sisters was Queen Elisabeth of the Belgians, consort of Albert I.

Marriage

On 10 July 1900 in Munich, Marie Gabrielle married her second cousin once-removed, Prince Rupprecht of Bavaria. He was the eldest son of Prince Ludwig of Bavaria (later Prince Regent and King of Bavaria) and Maria Theresia of Austria-Este. The wedding was attended by Prince Joachim of Prussia, representing his father Emperor Wilhelm II. After their marriage, the couple settled down in Bamberg, Bavaria, where Rupprecht was head of an army corps. Their two eldest children were born there.

The couple traveled a great deal. For example, they journeyed to Japan and returned by way of the United States in 1903. The trip to Japan was scientific in nature, and the couple were accompanied by a renowned professor from the University of Munich. Marie Gabrielle wrote home quite enthusiastically about their journey. Like her parents, she was a great lover of science and nature, as well as poetry and music.

While in Japan, Marie Gabrielle became seriously ill. Upon their return to Bavaria, she underwent surgery for appendicitis. She made a full recovery.

Bavarian succession

Rupprecht's grandfather, Luitpold, had become de facto ruler of Bavaria when King Ludwig II and his successor King Otto I both were declared insane in 1886. The constitution of Bavaria was amended on November 4, 1913 to include a clause specifying that if a regency by reason of incapacity lasted at least ten years, with no expectation that the King would ever be able to reign, the Regent could proclaim the end of the regency and assume the crown himself. The following day, King Otto I of Bavaria was deposed by Rupprecht's father, Prince Regent Ludwig, who then assumed the title King Ludwig III. The parliament assented on November 6, and Ludwig III took the constitutional oath on November 8. Rupprecht became the Crown Prince.

However, Marie Gabrielle had died from renal failure the previous year and never became Crown Princess of Bavaria. Her husband later remarried, to her first cousin Princess Antoinette of Luxembourg, on August 26, 1918.

Marie Gabrielle was interred at Theatinerkirche in Munich near her deceased children. Her only child to survive to adulthood was her second son Albrecht.

Issue

Princess Rupprecht of Bavaria with her three sons, Luitpold, Albrecht, and Rudolf, ca. 1912.

Name	Birth	Death	Note
By Rupprecht Maria Luitpold Ferdin Crown Prince of Bavaria (May 18, 18 August 2, 1955; married on July 10, 19 the Court Church in The Residenz, Mu			
Luitpold Maximilian Ludwig Karl of Bavaria	May 8, 1901	August 27, 1914	died child from
Irmingard Maria Therese José Cäcil-	September 21, 1902	April 21, 1903	died child from theri

ia Adelheid Michaela Antonia Adelgunde			
Albrecht Luitpold Ferdinand Michael	May 3, 1905	July 8, 1996	marri first, Coun Maria Drasl
von Trask marri secor 1971 Coun Marie Jenko Buzii	*Rudolf* Friedrich Rupprecht	May 30, 1909	June 26, 1912	had i died child from betes

Ancestry

Source http://en.wikipedia.org/wiki/Duchess_Marie_Gabrielle_in_Bavaria

Duchess Mathilde Ludovika in Bavaria

Princess Mathilde Ludovika
Countess of Trani

Mathilde Ludovika photographed circa 1870

Spouse	Prince Louis, Count of Trani
Issue	Princess Maria Teresa of Bourbon-Two Sicilies
House	House of Wittelsbach House of Bourbon-Two Sicilies
Father	Maximilian Joseph, Duke in Bavaria
Mother	Princess Ludovika of Bavaria
Born	30 September 1843 Possenhofen, Kingdom of Bavaria
Died	18 June 1925 (aged 81) Munich, Germany
Religion	Roman Catholic

Mathilde Ludovika, Duchess in Bavaria (30 September 1843 – 18 June 1925) was the fourth daughter of Maximilian, Duke in Bavaria and Princess Ludovika of Bavaria. Her mother was the youngest daughter King Maximilian I Joseph of Bavaria by his second wife Margravine Karoline of Baden.

Early life

Born and raised at Possenhofen Castle, Mathilde was a younger sister of (among others) Duke Karl-Theodor in Bavaria, Duchess Elisabeth in Bavaria and Duchess Marie Sophie in Bavaria. She was an older sister of (among others) Duchess Sophie in Bavaria.

Marriage & Family

On 5 June 1861, Mathilde married Lodovico, Count of Trani. He was Heir Presumptive to his older half-brother Francis II of the Two Sicilies. Francis was married to her older sister Marie Sophie. The bride was seventeen years old and the groom was twenty-two. They had a single daughter:
Princess Maria Teresa of Bourbon-Two Sicilies (15 January 1867 - 1 May 1909). She married Prince Wilhelm of Hohenzollern-Sigmaringen.

Two Sicilies Revolution

However the Two Sicilies were conquered by the Expedition of the Thousand under Giuseppe Garibaldi in 1861. Garibaldi served the Kingdom of Sardinia which was in the process of Italian unification.

Lodovico was still the heir of Francis as head of a deposed Royal House. He retained this position for the rest of his life but predeceased Francis on 8 June 1886. Francis was eventually succeeded by their younger brother Prince Alfonso, Count of Caserta. Mathilde survived her husband by thirty-nine years but never remarried.

Titles, styles, honours and arms

Titles and styles

30 September 1843 – 5 June 1861: *Her Royal Highness* Duchess Mathilde Ludovika in Bavaria

5 June 1861 – 8 June 1886: *Her Royal Highness* The Countess of Trani, Princess of Bourbon-Two Sicilies, Duchess in Bavaria

8 June 1886 – 18 June 1925: *Her Royal Highness* The Dowager Countess of Trani, Princess of Bourbon-Two Sicilies, Duchess in Bavaria

Ancestry

Source http://en.wikipedia.org/wiki/Duchess_Mathilde_Ludovika_in_Bavaria

Duchess Sophie Charlotte in Bavaria

Sophie Charlotte
Duchess of Alençon

Spouse Ferdinand d'Orléans
Issue
Louise, Princess of Bavaria
Emmanuel, Duke of Vendôme
House House of Orléans
House of Wittelsbach
Father Duke Maximilian Joseph in Bavaria
Mother Princess Ludovika of Bavaria
Born 23 February 1847
Possenhofen Castle, Possenhofen, Germany
Died 4 May 1897 (aged 50)
Paris, France

Duchess Sophie Charlotte Augustine in Bavaria (23 February 1847 – 4 May 1897) was a granddaughter-in-law of King Louis-Philippe of France, the favourite sister of Empress Elisabeth of Austria and fiancée of King Ludwig II of Bavaria..

Biography

Sophie Charlotte was born at the Possenhofen Castle, the residence of her paternal family, Dukes in Bavaria. She was a daughter of Duke Maximilian Joseph in Bavaria (1808–1888) and Princess Ludovika of Bavaria. The ninth of ten children born to her parents, she was known as *Sopherl* within the family.

She was also a sister of Empress Elisabeth of Austria and Queen Maria Sophia of the Two Sicilies. After the marriage of her older sister, Duchess Mathilde Ludovika in Bavaria to 1861 to the Neapolitan Prince Luis of the Two Sicilies, her parents then looked for a suitable husband for Sophie Charlotte.

She was engaged to her cousin King Ludwig II of Bavaria. Their engagement was publicised on 22 January 1867, but after having repeatedly postponed the wedding date, Ludwig finally cancelled it in October. For details of the situation see the article on Edgar Hanfstaengl.

Other proposed husbands included the renowned homosexual Archduke Ludwig Viktor of Austria, brother of both Franz Josef I of Austria and Maximilian I of Mexico, as well as the future Luís I of Portugal. Another candidate was Duke Philipp of Württemberg, the first cousin of her eventual husband.

She refused all the candidates. She was sent to stay with her aunt, Amalie Auguste of Bavaria, then the Queen of Saxony as wife of John of Saxony. It was in Saxony Sophie Charlotte met Ferdinand d'Orléans (12 July 1844 – 29 June 1910), *Duke of Alençon* and grandson of the late Louis Philippe I (died 1850). Soon after, on 28 September 1868 she married the Duke of Alençon, son of Louis d'Orléans, at Possenhofen Castle near Starnberg.

She had a good relationship with her husband as well as with her sister-in-law Marguerite Adélaïde d'Orléans, wife of Władysław Czartoryski. Her mother in law, Victoria of Saxe-Coburg-Kohary, cousin of Queen Victoria, had died in 1857. Sophie Charlotte did not have an overly good relationship with her father-in-law, the widowed Duke of Nemours.

The year after their marriage, the ducal couple moved to Teddington, London England, where Sophie Charlotte gave birth to her first child, Louise d'Orléans, at Bushy House.

Sophie died in a fire at the Bazar de la Charité in Paris on 4 May 1897. She had refused rescue attempts, insisting that the girls working with her at the bazaar be saved first.

Issue

Louise Victoire Marie Amélie Sophie d'Orléans (19 July 1869 – 4 February 1952) married Prince Alfons of Bavaria (1862–1933) and had issue; (the line ended in dynastical sense in 1990 in male line, with cognatic descendants still present).

Philippe Emmanuel Maximilien Marie Eudes d'Orléans, *Duke of Vendôme* (18 January 1872 – 1 February 1931) married Princess Henriette of Belgium and had issue (the line ended dynastically in 1970 in male line, with cognatic descendants still present).

Ancestry

Titles, styles, honours and arms

Titles and styles

23 February 1847 – 28 September 1868 *Her Royal Highness* Duchess Sophie Charlotte in Bavaria
28 September 1868 – 4 May 1897 *Her Royal Highness* The Duchess of Alençon
Source http://en.wikipedia.org/wiki/Duchess_Sophie_Charlotte_in_Bavaria

Dukes in Bavaria

Duke in Bavaria (German: *Herzog in Bayern*) was a title used among others since 1506, when primogeniture was established, by all members of the House of Wittelsbach, with the exception of the Duke *of* Bavaria which began to be a unique position. So reads for instance the full title of Karl I, Count Palatine of Zweibrücken-Birkenfeld and patriarch of the House of Palatinate-Birkenfeld: "Count Palatine by Rhine, Duke in Bavaria, Count to Veldenz and Sponheim". The title grew in importance as Wilhelm, Count Palatine of Zweibrücken-Birkenfeld-Gelnhausen began to use it as his primary title. This choice has also had effect for his descendants.

Since 1799

On 16 February 1799, the head of the House of Wittelsbach Charles Theodore of Bavaria died without issue. Wittelsbach had been the ruling house of Bavaria since 1180 with the title of a Duke of Bavaria, and the higher title of an Elector of the Holy Roman Empire since 1648. As after the Landshut War of Succession primogeniture was established, there could only be one Duke of Bavaria anymore, resulting in the actually quite unprecedented decision to create a title of Duke *in* Bavaria for the rest of the family, which all members of the House took for themselves, even the older Palatine branch – the other major Wittelsbach possession. Reversely, all Wittelbachs were also Counts Palatine by Rhine. After Charles Theodore's death, who had unified Bavaria with the Palatinate and the other major possessions of Jülich and Berg in his person, two cadet branches were surviving: one headed by Maximilian I Joseph, Count Palatine of Zweibrücken, the other by William, Count Palatine of Gelnhausen, and both Zweibrücken and Gelnhausen were occupied by the French, which might explain why the custom was abandoned to name cadet branches by the title of their cadet possessions no matter how small.

The both agreed in the House Treaty of Ansbach that the Wittelsbach inheritances should be indivisible further on. Maximilian Joseph, as from the senior branch, inherited Charles Theodor's title of Elector of Bavaria, while William, his brother-in-law in addition to rather distinct a relative, was compensated with the title of Duke *in* Bavaria. As head of a specific family branch, it is possible since to speak somewhat paradoxically of *The Duke in* Bavaria. When Wittelsbach became a Royal House, the Dukes in Bavaria were lifted to the dignity of a Royal Highness. Then if not earlier, the title of Duke in Bavaria came into formal disuse by the Royal branch, who were quite content to be Princes of Bavaria. It should be kept in mind that even if we commonly speak of a Royal and a Ducal branch of the House, it was clear that the Dukes as well were of royal rank, and to make things more complicated, the head of the royal branch is now again called the Duke: the Duke *of* Bavaria, of course. Among the notable members of the Ducal branch were Duke Max, who, a talented Zither player and composer himself, ranks among the most important promoters of Bavarian folk-music; his daughters Empress Elisabeth of Austria, Queen of Hungary and Queen Mary Sophie of the Two Sicilies; and in more recent times Sophie, Hereditary Princess of Liechtenstein.

In 1965 there were only two male members of the family, Duke Ludwig Wilhelm and his cousin Duke Luitpold; both were elderly and had no children. On 18 March 1965 Duke Ludwig Wilhelm adopted Prince Max of Bavaria, the second son of Albrecht, Duke of Bavaria and the grandson of Ludwig Wilhelm's sister Marie Gabrielle. From this point onwards Max has used the surname "Herzog in Bayern" in place of the surname "Prinz von Bayern". Max has five daughters, including the Sophie mentioned already, all of whom were born with the surname "Herzogin in Bayern".

Ancestors

Wilhelm, the first Duke in Bavaria, was descended from the line of *Palatinate-Zweibrücken-Birkenfeld-Gelnhausen*. His ancestors were:
Wolfgang, Count Palatine of Zweibrücken (1526–1569), m. Anna of Hesse.
Karl I, Count Palatine of Zweibrücken-Birkenfeld (1560–1600), fifth son of Wolfgang, m. Dorothea of Brunswick-Lüneburg
Christian I, Count Palatine of Zweibrücken-Bischweiler (1598–1654), third son of Karl, m. his cousin Magdalene Catherine of Zweibrücken, a daughter of John II, Count Palatine of Zweibrücken and Cathérine de Rohan.
John Charles, Count Palatine of Gelnhausen (1638–1704), second surviving son of Christian I, m. Esther Marie of Witzleben. They were parents of several sons.
John, Count Palatine of Gelnhausen (1698–1780), second son of John Charles, m. Sophie Charlotte of Salm-Dhaun, father of William, Duke in Bavaria.

Dukes in Bavaria

If we take 1799 as the beginning of somewhat a House of its own, the heads of this house were:
William (1789/99-1837), (The) Count Palatine of Gelnhausen 1789, Duke in Bavaria (roughly) 1799
Pius August (1837)
Max Joseph (1837–1888)
Charles Theodore (1888–1909) due to abdication of his elder brother on account of his morganatic marriage
Louis William (1909–1968)
After his death, his cousin Luitpold Emanuel (lived 1890-1973) remained the last natural member of the family.
Max Emanuel, adopted, since 1968.
The members of the family used the title Duke or Duchess in Bavaria, with the style of Royal Highness.

Family tree

Wilhelm (1752–1837), second son of Johann, m. 1780 Countess Palatine Maria Anna of Birkenfeld (1753–1824), and had issue:
Maria Elisabeth Amalie Franziska (1784-1849), m. 1808 Louis Alexandre Berthier, sovereign Prince of Neuchâtel (1753-1815), and had issue.
Pius August (1786-1837), m. 1807 Princess and Duchess Amélie Louise of Arenberg (1789-1823), and had issue:
Maximilian Joseph (1808-1888), m. 1828 Princess Ludovika of Bavaria (1808-1892) and had issue:
Ludwig Wilhelm (1831-1920), left morganatic issue through his surviving daughters.
Wilhelm Karl (1832-1833).
Helene (1834-1890), m. 1858 Maximilian Anton Lamoral, Hereditary Prince of Thurn and Taxis (1831-1867) and had issue.
Elisabeth (1837-1898), m. 1854 Emperor Franz Josef of Austria (1830-1916) and had issue.
Karl Theodor (1839-1909), m. 1865

Princess Sophie of Saxony (1845-1867) and had issue:
Amalie Marie (1865-1912), m. 1892 Duke Wilhelm of Urach (1864-1928) and had issue.
m. secondly 1874 Infanta Maria Josefa of Portugal (1857-1943) and had further issue:
Sophie (1875-1957), m. 1898 Count Hans Viet of Toerring-Jettenbach (1862-1929) and had issue.
Elisabeth (1876-1965), m. 1900 King Albert I of the Belgians (1875-1934) and had issue.
Marie Gabrielle (1878-1912), m. 1900 Crown Prince Rupprecht of Bavaria (1869-1955) and had issue.
Ludwig Wilhelm (1884-1968), m. 1917 Princess Eleonore of Sayn-Wittgenstein-Berleburg (1880-1965); in 1965 he adopted:
Prince Max of Bavaria (born 1937), grandson of Marie Gabrielle, who thereby became Duke in Bavaria; he m. 1967 Countess Elizabeth Douglas (born 1940) and has issue:
Sophie (born 1967), m. 1993 Hereditary Prince Alois of Liechtenstein (born 1968) and has issue.
Marie Caroline (born 1969), m. 1991 Duke Philipp of Württemberg (born 1964) and has issue.
Helene (born 1972).
Elizabeth (born 1973), m. 2004 Dr. Daniel Terberger (born 1967) and has issue.
Anna (born 1975), m. 2007 Klaus Runow (born 1964).
Franz Josef (1888-1912).
Maria Sophie (1841-1925), m. 1859 King Francesco II of the Two Sicilies (1836-1894) and had issue.
Mathilde Ludovika (1843-1925), m. 1861 Prince Lodovico of the Two Sicilies, Count of Trani (1838-1886) and had issue.
Sophie Charlotte (1847-1897), m. 1868 Prince Ferdinand of Orléans, Duke of Alençon (1844-1910) and had issue.
Maximilian Emanuel (1849-1893), m. 1875 Princess Amalie of Saxe-Coburg and Gotha (1848-1894) and had issue:
Siegfried (1876-1952).
Christoph (1879-1963), m. 1924 Anna Sibig (1874-1958).
Luitpold (1898-1973).

Homes

The notable properties of the family are/were: Banz Abbey and Tegernsee Abbey

Source http://en.wikipedia.org/wiki/Dukes_in_Bavaria

Elisabeth of Bavaria, Queen of Belgium

Elisabeth of Bavaria

Photo of Elisabeth
Queen consort of the Belgians
Tenure 17 December 1909 – 17 February 1934
Spouse Albert I of Belgium
Issue
Leopold III of Belgium
Prince Charles, Count of Flanders
Marie-José, Queen of Italy
Full name
Elisabeth Gabriele Valérie Marie
House	House of Saxe-Coburg and Gotha
	House of Wittelsbach
Father	Duke Karl-Theodor in Bavari
Mother	Infanta Maria Josepha of Portgal
Born	25 July 1876
	Possenhofen Castle, Kingdom of Bavaria
Died	23 November 1965 (aged 89)
	Brussels, Belgium
Burial	Church of Our Lady of Laeke

Duchess Elisabeth in Bavaria (born *Elisabeth Gabriele Valérie Marie, Duchess in Bavaria*) (25 July 1876 – 23 November 1965) was Queen of the Belgians as the spouse of King Albert I. She was the mother of King Leopold III of Belgium and of Queen Marie José of Italy, and grandmother of kings Baudouin and Albert II of Belgium.

Family

Born in Possenhofen Castle, her father was Karl-Theodor, Duke in Bavaria, head of a cadet branch of the Bavarian royal family, and an ophthalmologist of recognized reputation. She was named in honor of her father's sister, Empress Elisabeth of Austria, better known as Sisi. Her mother was Maria Josepha of Portugal, daughter of exiled Miguel I of Portugal.

An artist himself, Duke Karl-Theodor cultivated the artistic tastes of his family and Elisabeth was raised with a deep love for painting, music and sculpture. At her father's clinic, where her mother assisted her father as a nurse, Elisabeth obtained exposure to productive labour and to human suffering unusual at that time for a princess.

Married life

In Munich on 2 October 1900, Duchess Elisabeth married Prince Albert, second-in-line to the throne of Belgium (after his father Prince Philippe, Count of Flanders). Upon her husband's accession to the Belgian throne in 1909, Elisabeth became queen. The city of Élisabethville, today Lubumbashi, in the Congo was named in her honour.

At the time that Albert and Elisabeth met, Prince Albert was the heir to his uncle Leopold II of the Belgians. Albert was the second son of Prince Philippe, Count of Flanders and Princess Marie of Hohenzollern-Sigmaringen, a sister of King Carol I of Romania.

Engagement photo of Elisabeth and Albert.

At birth, Albert occupied the third place in the line of succession behind his father and elder brother, Prince Baudouin. The unexpected death of Baudouin in January 1891 immediately raised Albert to prominence within his country. A studious, quiet man, Albert was not the choice of heir that King Leopold II would have relished. As the only living male member of his generation, Albert was guaranteed the Crown of the Belgians upon the King's death. Albert had two sisters who survived into adulthood, Princess Henriette who married Prince Emmanuel of Orléans, and Princess Josephine who married her cousin, Prince Karl-Anton of Hohenzollern-Sigmaringen, brother of King Ferdinand I of Romania.

During the First World War, she and the King resided in De Panne. The Queen made herself beloved by visiting the front lines and by sponsoring a nursing unit. Despite her German background, she was a popular queen, perceived as eagerly supporting her adoptive country.

From September 23 till November 13, 1919, the Queen, together with the King and Prince Léopold, undertook an official visit to the United States of America. During a journey in the historic pueblo of Isleta in New Mexico, the King awarded the Order of Léopold to Father Anton Docher, As a memento, the King was given a turquoise cross mounted in silver made by the Tiwa people. 10 000 persons journeyed to Isleta for the occasion.

The Queen (in a white dress) and the King during their visit in Isleta pueblo New Mexico 1919 with Anton Docher

Later years

In 1934, Albert I died in a climbing accident in the Ardennes of Belgium, near Namur. Elisabeth lived to see her son become king (but also go into exile and abdicate), her younger son become, effectively, regent of the realm, and her grandson mount the throne.

As queen dowager, she became a patron of the arts and was known for her friendship with such notable scientists as Albert Einstein. During the German occupation of Belgium from 1940 to 1944, she used her influence as queen and German connections to assist in the rescue of hundreds of Jewish children from deportation by the Nazis. When Brussels was liberated, she allowed her palace to be used for headquarters of the British XXX Corps, and presented its commander General Horrocks with its mascot, a young wild boar named 'Chewing Gum'. After the war she was awarded the title Righteous Among the Nations by the Israeli government.

During the 1950s, the Queen evoked controversy abroad by visiting the Soviet Union, China and Poland, trips that prompted some to label her as the "Red Queen."

Queen Elisabeth died in Brussels at the age of 89 on 23 November 1965. She is interred in the royal vault at the Church of Our Lady of Laeken, Brussels. She was the 1,016th Dame of the Royal Order of Queen Maria Luisa.

Children

Léopold Philippe Charles Albert Meinrad Hubertus Marie Miguel, Duke of Brabant, Prince of Belgium, who became later the fourth king of the Belgians (as Leopold III), born 3 November 1901, and died at Woluwe-Saint-Lambert on 25 September 1983.
Charles-Théodore Henri Antoine Meinrad, Count of Flanders, Prince of Belgium, Regent of Belgium, born Brussels 10 October 1903, and died at Ostend on 1 June 1983.
Marie-José Charlotte Sophie Amélie Henriette Gabrielle, Princess of Belgium, born Ostend 4 August 1906. She was married at Rome, Italy, on 8 January 1930 to Prince Umberto Nicola Tomasso Giovanni Maria, Prince of Piedmont, born on 15 September 1904, and died on 18 March 1983, at Geneva, Switzerland. He became King Umberto II of Italy on 9 May 1946. Marie-José died 27 January 2001.

Titles and styles

25 July 1876 – 2 October 1900: *Her Royal Highness* Duchess Elisabeth in Bavaria
2 October 1900 – 17 December 1909: *Her Royal Highness* Princess Elisabeth of Belgium
17 December 1909 – 17 February 1934: *Her Majesty* The Queen of the Belgians
17 February 1934 – 23 November 1965: *Her Majesty* Queen Elisabeth of Belgium

Ancestry

Source http://en.wikipedia.org/wiki/Elisabeth_of_Bavaria,_Queen_of_Belgium

Empress Elisabeth of Austria

Elisabeth of Austria

A photograph of Elisabeth on the day o coronation as Queen of Hungary, 8 Jun 1867

Empress consort of Austria; Apostolic queen consort of Hunga Queen consort of Bohemia and Cro

Tenure	24 April 1854 – 10 Septer 1898
Coronation	8 June 1867
Spouse	Franz Joseph I of Austria

Issue
Archduchess Sophie
Archduchess Gisela
Rudolf, Crown Prince of Austria
Archduchess Marie-Valerie

Full name
Elisabeth Amalie Eugenie

House	House of Habsburg-Lorra House of Wittelsbach
Father	Duke Maximilian Joseph Bavaria
Mother	Princess Ludovika of Bav
Born	24 December 1837 Munich, Kingdom of Bav (now part of Germany)
Died	10 September 1898 (aged Geneva, Switzerland (ass nated)
Religion	Roman Catholic

Elisabeth of Austria (24 December 1837 – 10 September 1898) was the wife of Franz Joseph I, and therefore both Empress of Austria and Queen of Hungary. She also held the titles of Queen of Bohemia and Croatia, among others. From an early age, she was called *Sisi* by family and friends.

Although Elisabeth had a limited (but significant) influence on Austro-Hungarian politics, she became an historical icon. The Empress is now thought to have been a non-conformist who abhorred conventional court protocol, as well as a free spirit, who valued an individual sense of freedom above anything else. Following the suicide of her son Rudolf, she withdrew from public life. She was murdered by an anarchist in Geneva, Switzerland in 1898. Elisabeth is the longest serving consort of Austria.

Duchess in Bavaria

Elisabeth at 11 years, her brother Karl Theodor, Duke in Bavaria, and their dog "Bummerl" at Possenhofen Castle

Born **Her Royal Highness Duchess Elisabeth Amalie Eugenie** on 24 December 1837 in Munich, Bavaria, she was the fourth child of Duke Maximilian Joseph in Bavaria and Princess Ludovika of Bavaria. Maximilian was considered to be rather peculiar; he had a childish love of circuses and traveled the Bavarian countryside to escape his duties. The family home was at Possenhofen Castle, far from the protocols of court. "Sisi" and her brothers and sisters grew up in a very unrestrained and unstructured environment, she often skipped her lessons to go riding about the countryside.

In 1853, Princess Sophie of Bavaria, the domineering mother of 23-year-old Emperor Francis Joseph, preferring to have a niece as a daughter-in-law rather than a stranger, arranged a marriage between her son and her sister Ludovika's eldest daughter, Helene. Although the couple had never met, Franz Joseph's obedience was taken for granted by the archduchess, who once was described as "the only man in the Hofburg" for her authoritarian manner. The Duchess and Helene were invited to journey to resort of Bad Ischl, Upper Austria to receive his formal proposal of marriage. Fifteen-year-old Sisi accompanied her mother and sister and they traveled from Munich in several coaches. They arrived late as the Duchess, prone to migraine, had to interrupt the journey and the coach with their gala dresses never did arrive. The family was still in mourning over the death of an aunt so they were dressed in black and unable to change to more suitable clothing before meeting the young Emperor. While black did not suit eighteen-year-old Helene's dark coloring, it made her younger sister's blonder looks more striking by contrast.

Helene was a pious, quiet young woman, and she and Franz Joseph felt ill at ease in each other's company, but Franz Joseph was instantly infatuated with Elisabeth. He did not propose to Helene, but defied his mother and informed her that if he could not have Elisabeth, he would not marry at all. Five days later their betrothal was officially announced. The couple were married eight months later in Vienna at the Augustinerkirche on 24 April 1854.

Empress

The young Elisabeth shortly after becoming Austrian Empress (by Amanda Bergstedt, 1855)

After enjoying an informal and unstructured childhood, Elisabeth, who was shy and introverted by nature, and more so among the stifling formality of Habsburg court life, had difficulty adapting to the Hofburg and its rigid protocols and strict etiquette. Within a few weeks, Elisabeth started to display health problems: she had fits of coughing and became anxious and frightened whenever she had to descend a narrow steep staircase.

She was surprised to find she was pregnant and gave birth to her first child, a daughter, Archduchess Sophie of Austria (1855–1857), just ten months after her wedding. Princess Sophie, who often referred to Elisabeth as a "silly young mother", not only named the child (after herself) without consulting the mother, but took complete charge of the baby, refusing to allow Elisabeth to breastfeed or otherwise care for her own child. When a second daughter, Archduchess Gisela of Austria (1856–1932), was born a year later, she took her away from Elisabeth as well.

The fact that she had not produced a male heir made Elisabeth feel more unwanted than ever in the palace. One day she found a pamphlet on her desk with the following words underlined:

...The natural destiny of a Queen is to give an heir to the throne. If the Queen is so fortunate as to provide the State with a Crown-Prince this should be the end of her ambition – she should by no means meddle with the government of an Empire, the care of which is not a task for women... If the Queen bears no sons, she is merely a foreigner in the State, and a very dangerous foreigner, too. For as she can never hope to be looked on kindly here, and must always expect to be sent back whence she came, so will she always seek to win the King by other than natural means; she will struggle for position and power by intrigue and the sowing of discord, to the mischief of the King, the nation, and the Empire...

Her mother-in-law is generally considered to be the source of the malicious pamphlet. The accusation of political meddling referred to Elisabeth's influence on her husband regarding his Italian and Hungarian subjects. When she traveled to Italy with him she persuaded him to show mercy toward political prisoners. In 1857 Elisabeth visited Hungary for the first time with her husband and two daughters, and it left a deep and lasting impression upon her, probably because in Hungary she found a welcome respite from the constraints of Austrian court life. It was "the first time that Elisabeth had met with men of character in Franz Joseph's realm, and she became acquainted with an aristocratic independence that scorned to hide its sentiments behind courtly forms of speech... She felt her innermost soul reach out in sympathy to the proud, steadfast people of this land..." Unlike the archduchess, who despised the Magyars, Elisabeth felt such an affinity for them that she began to learn Hungarian; the country reciprocated in its adoration of her.

This same trip proved tragic as both of Elisabeth's children became ill with diarrhea. While Gisela recovered quickly, two-year-old Sophie grew steadily weaker, then died. It is generally assumed today that she died of typhus. Her death pushed Elisabeth, who was already prone to bouts of melancholy, into periods of heavy depression, which would haunt her for the rest of her life. She turned away from her living daughter, began neglecting her, and their relationship never recovered.

In December 1857 Elisabeth became pregnant for the third time in as many years, and her mother, who had been concerned about her daughter's physical and mental health, hoped that this new pregnancy would help her recover.

Physical regimen

Equestrian portrait of Elisabeth at Possenhofen Castle, 1853

At 172 cm (5 feet 8 inches), Elisabeth was unusually tall (she was taller than her husband); even after four pregnancies she maintained her weight at approximately 50 kg (110 pounds) for the rest of her life. She achieved this through fasting and exercise. Elisabeth was strongly attached to her parents, especially to her mother, and was still a child in search of an identity of her own when an adult role with unusual obligations and restrictions was imposed upon her. She had no control in her new life and was unable to identify herself as both the spouse of the emperor and a young mother. As a result, she attempted to recreate her childhood with its lack of obligations. The only quality for which she felt herself appreciated, and over which she had control, was her physical appearance, so she started cultivating this as the primary source of her self-esteem. Obsessively achievement-oriented and almost compulsively perfectionistic in her attitudes, she became a slave to her own beauty and image.

In deep mourning after her daughter Sophie's death, Elisabeth refused to eat for days; a behavior that would reappear in later periods of melancholy and depression. Whereas she previously had supper with the family, she now began to avoid this; and if she did eat with them, she ate quickly and very little. Whenever her weight threatened to exceed fifty kilos, a "fasting cure" or "hunger cure" would follow, which involved almost complete fasting. Meat itself often filled her with disgust, so she either had the juice of half-raw beefsteaks squeezed into a thin soup, or else adhered to a diet of milk and eggs.

Elisabeth emphasised her extreme slenderness through the practice of "tight-lacing". During the peak period of 1859-60, which coincided with Franz-Joseph's political and military defeats in Italy, her sexual withdrawal from her husband after three pregnancies in rapid succession, and her losing battle with her mother-in-law for dominance in rearing her children, she reduced her waist to 16 inches in circumference. Corsets of the time were split-busk types, fastening up the front with hooks and eyes, but Elisabeth had more rigid, solid-front ones made in Paris out of leather, "like those of Parisian courtesans", probably to hold up under the stress of such strenuous lacing, "a proceeding which sometimes took quite an hour". The fact that "she only wore them for a few weeks" may indicate that even leather proved inadequate for her needs. Elisabeth's defiant flaunting of this exaggerated dimension angered her mother-in-law, who expected her to be pregnant continuously.

Although on her return to Vienna in August 1862, a lady-in-waiting reported that "she eats properly, sleeps well, and does not tight-lace anymore", her clothing from this time until her death still measured only 18 1/2 – 19 1/2 inches around the waist, which prompted the Prince of Hesse to describe her as "almost inhumanly slender." She developed a horror of fat women and transmitted this attitude to her youngest daughter, who was terrified when, as a little girl, she first met Queen Victoria.

In her youth Elisabeth followed the fashions of the age, which for many years were cage-crinolined hoop skirts, but when fashion began to change, she was at the forefront of abandoning the hoop skirt for a tighter and leaner silhouette. She disliked both expensive accoutrements and the protocol that dictated constant changes of clothing, preferring simple, monochromatic riding habit-like attire. She never wore petticoats or any other "underlinen", as they added bulk, and was often literally sewn into her clothes, to bypass waistbands, creases, and wrinkles and to further emphasize the "wasp waist" that became her hallmark.

The empress developed extremely rigorous and disciplined exercise habits. Every castle she lived in was equipped with a gymnasium, the Knights' Hall of the Hofburg was converted into one, mats and balance beams were installed in her bedchamber so that she could practice on them each morning, and the imperial villa at Ischl was fitted with gigantic mirrors so that she could correct every movement and position. She took up fencing in her 50s with equal discipline. A fervent horsewoman, she rode every day for hours on end, becoming probably the world's best, as well as best-known, female equestrian at the time. When due to gout, she could no longer endure long hours in the saddle, she substituted walking, subjecting her attendants to interminable marches and hiking tours in all weather.

In the last years of her life, Elisabeth became even more restless and obsessive, weighing herself up to three times a day. She regularly took steam baths to prevent weight gain; by 1894 she had wasted away to near emaciation, reaching her lowest point of 95.7 lbs (43.5 kg). There were some aberrations in Elisabeth's diet that appear to be signs of binge eating, On one occasion in 1878 the Empress astonished her travelling companions when she unexpectedly visited a restaurant incognito, where she drank champagne, ate a broiled chicken, an Italian salad, and finished with a "considerable quantity of cake". She may have satisfied her urge to binge in secret on other occasions; in 1881 she purchased an English country house and had a spiral staircase built from her living room into the kitchen, so that she could reach it in private.

Beauty

Portrait of Elisabeth depicting her long hair (by Franz Xaver Winterhalter, 1864), one of two so-called "intimate" portraits of the empress; although its existence was kept a secret from the general public, it was the emperor's favourite portrait of her and kept opposite his desk in his private study

In addition to her rigorous exercise routines Elisabeth practised what could be called a true beauty cult, but one that was highly ascetic, solitary, and prone to bizarre, eccentric, and almost mystic routines. Daily care of her abundant and extremely long hair, which in the time turned from the dark blonde of her youth, to chestnut brown, took at least three hours. Her hair was so long and heavy that she often complained that the weight of the elaborate double braids and pins gave her headaches. Her hairdresser, Franziska Feifalik, was originally a stage hairdresser at the Wiener Burgtheater. Responsible for all of Elisabeth's ornate hairstyles, she always accompanied her on her wanderings.

Feifalik was forbidden to wear rings and required to wear white gloves; after hours of dressing, braiding, and pinning up the Empress' tresses, the hairs that fell out had to be presented in a silver bowl to her reproachful empress for inspection. When her hair was washed with special "essences" of eggs and cognac once every two weeks, all activities and obligations were cancelled for that day. Before her son's death, she tasked Feifalik with tweezing gray hairs away, but at the end of her life her hair was described as "abundant, though streaked with silver threads."

Elisabeth used these captive hours during grooming to learn languages; she spoke fluent English and French, and added modern Greek to her Hungarian studies. Her Greek tutor described the ritual:

"Hairdressing takes almost two hours, she said, and while my hair is busy, my mind stays idle. I am afraid that my mind escapes through the hair and onto the fingers of my hairdresser. Hence my headache afterwards. The Empress sat at a table which was moved to the middle of the room and covered with a white cloth. She was shrouded in a white, laced peignoir, her hair, unfastened and reaching to the floor, enfolded her entire body."

Unlike other women of her time, Elisabeth used little cosmetics or perfume, as she wished to showcase her "natural" beauty, but she tested countless beauty products prepared in the court pharmacy, or prepared by a lady-in-waiting in her own apartments, to preserve it. Although one favorite, "Crème Céleste", was compounded from white wax, spermaceti, sweet almond oil, and rosewater; she attached far less importance to creams and emolients, and experimented with a wide variety of facial tonics and waters, from which she apparently expected more results. Elisabeth slept without a pillow on a metal bedstead, all the better to retain her upright posture, with either raw veal or crushed strawberries lining her nightly leather facial mask. She was heavily massaged and often slept with cloths soaked in either violet- or cider-vinegar above her hips to preserve her slim waist, and her neck was wrapped with cloths soaked in Kummerfeld-toned washing water. To further preserve her skin tone, she took both a cold shower every morning (which in later years aggravated her arthritis) and an olive oil bath in the evening.

After age thirty-two, she did not sit for any more portraits, and would not allow any photographs of her to be taken, so that her public image of the eternal beauty would not be challenged. The few photographs that were taken without her knowledge show a woman who was "graceful, but almost too slender".

Marriage

Engraving depicting the Hungarian royal family at Gödöllő Palace (circa 1870)

Franz Joseph was passionately in love with his wife, but later she did not reciprocate his feelings fully and increasingly felt stifled by the court etiquette. He was an unimaginative and sober man, a political reactionary who was still guided by his mother and her adherence to the strict Spanish Court Ceremonial ("Spanisches Hofzeremoniell") regarding both his public and domestic life, whereas Elisabeth inhabited a different world altogether. Restless to the point of hyperactivity, naturally introverted, and emotionally distant from her husband, she fled him as well as her duties of life at court, avoiding them both as much as she could. He indulged her wanderings, but constantly and unsuccessfully tried to tempt her into a more domestic life with him.

Elisabeth slept very little and spent hours reading and writing at night, and even took up smoking, a shocking habit for women which made her the further subject of already avid gossip. She had a special interest in history, philosophy, and literature, and developed a profound reverence for the German lyric poet and radical political thinker, Heinrich Heine, whose letters she collected.

She tried to make a name for herself by writing Heine-inspired poetry. Referring to herself as Titania, Shakespeare's Fairy Queen, Elisabeth expressed her intimate thoughts and desires in a large number of romantic poems, which served as a type of secret diary. Most of her poetry relates to her journeys, classical Greek and romantic themes, and ironic commentary on the Habsburg dynasty. Her wanderlust is defined by her own work:

O'er thee, like thine own sea birds// I'll circle without rest//For me earth holds no corner//To build a lasting nest.

Elisabeth was an emotionally complex woman, and perhaps due to the melancholy and eccentricity that was considered a given characteristic of her Wittelsbach lineage (the best-known member of the family being her favorite cousin, the eccentric Ludwig II of Bavaria), she was interested in the treatment of the mentally ill. In 1871 when the Emperor asked her what she would like as a gift for her Saint's Day, she listed a young tiger and a medallion, but: "...a fully equipped lunatic asylum would please me most".

Birth of a son

On 21 August 1858, Elisabeth finally gave birth to an heir, Rudolf (1858–1889). The 101-gun salute announcing the welcome news to Vienna also signaled an increase in her influence at court. This, combined with her sympathy toward Hungary, made Elisabeth an ideal mediator between the Magyars and the emperor. Her interest in politics had developed as she matured; she was liberal, and placed herself decisively on the Hungarian side in the increasing conflict of nationalities within the empire.

Elisabeth was a personal advocate for Hungarian Count Gyula Andrássy, who also was rumored to be her lover. Whenever difficult negotiations broke off between the Hungarians and the court, they were resumed with her help. During these protracted dealings, Elisabeth suggested to the emperor that Andrássy be made the Premier of Hungary as part of a compromise, and in a forceful attempt to bring the two men together, strongly admonished her husband:

I have just had an interview with Andrássy. He set forth his views clearly and plainly. I quite understood them and arrived at the conclusion that if you would trust him – and trust him entirely – we might still be saved, not only Hungary, but the monarchy, too.... I can assure you that you are not dealing with a man desirous of playing a part at any price or striving for a position; on the contrary, he is risking his present position, which is a fine one. But approaching shipwreck, he, too, is prepared to do all in his power to save it; what he possesses – his understanding and influence in the country – he will lay at your feet. For the last time I beg you in Rudolf's name not to lose this, at the last moment... ...If you say 'No,' if at the last moment you are no longer willing to listen to disinterested counsels. then... you will be relieved forever from my future... and nothing will remain to me but the consciousness that whatever may happen, I shall be able to say honestly to Rudolf one day; "I did everything in my power. Your misfortunes are not on my conscience."

When Elisabeth still was blocked from controlling her son's upbringing and education, she openly rebelled. Due to her nervous attacks, fasting cures, severe exercise regime, and frequent fits of coughing, the state of her health had become so alarming that in October 1860 she was reported to suffer not only from "green-sickness" (anemia), but also from physical exhaustion. A serious lung complaint of "Lungenschwindsucht" (tuberculosis) was feared by Dr. Skoda, a lung specialist, who advised a stay on Madeira. During this time the court was rife with malicious rumors that Franz Joseph was having a liaison with an actress named Frau Roll, leading to speculation today, that Elisabeth's symptoms could have been anything from psychosomatic to a result of venereal disease.

Elisabeth seized on the excuse and left her husband and children, to spend the winter in seclusion. Six months later, a mere four days after her return to Vienna, she again experienced coughing fits and fever. She ate hardly anything and slept badly, and Dr. Skoda observed a recurrence of her lung disease. A fresh rest cure was advised, this time on Corfu, where she improved almost immediately. If her illnesses were psychosomatic, abating when she was removed from her husband and her duties, her eating habits were causing physical problems as well. In 1862 she had not seen Vienna for a year when her family physician, Dr. Fischer of Munich, examined her and observed serious anemia and signs of "dropsy" (edema). Her feet were sometimes so swollen that she could walk only laboriously, and with the support of others. On medical advice, she went to Bad Kissingen for a cure. Elisabeth recovered quickly at the spa, but instead of returning home to assuage the gossip about her absence she spent more time with her own family in Bavaria. In August 1862, after a two-year absence, she returned shortly before her husband's birthday, but immediately suffered from a violent "migraine" and vomited four times en route, which supports the theory that her primary complaints were stress-related and psychosomatic.

Rudolf was now four years old, and Franz Joseph hoped for another son to safeguard the succession. Dr. Fischer claimed that the health of the empress would not permit another pregnancy, and she would regularly have to go to Kissingen for a cure. Elisabeth fell into her old pattern of escaping boredom and dull court protocol through frequent walking and riding, using her health as an excuse to avoid both official obligations and sexual intimacy. Her successful avoidance of further pregnancies would have been a natural reaction to having been assigned the role of an imperial brood mare, bearing a child a year only to have it taken away from her, but the importance of preserving her youthful appearance was an important influence in her decision:

"Children are the curse of a woman, for when they come, they drive away Beauty, which is the best gift of the gods".

She was now more assertive in her defiance of her husband and mother-in-law than before, openly opposing them on the subject of the military education of Rudolf, who, like his mother, was extremely sensitive and not suited to the life at court.

Hungarian coronation

Coronation of Franz Joseph and Elisabeth as King and Queen of Hungary and Croatia

Photograph of Elisabeth as Queen of Hungary (by Emil Rabending, 1867)

After having used every excuse to avoid pregnancy, Elisabeth later decided that she wanted a fourth child. Her decision was at once a deliberate personal choice and a political negotiation: by returning to the marriage, she ensured that Hungary, with which she felt an intense emotional alliance, would gain an equal footing with Austria.

The Austro-Hungarian Compromise of 1867 created the double monarchy of

Austro–Hungary. Andrassy was made the first Hungarian prime minister and in return, he saw that Franz Joseph and Elisabeth were officially crowned King and Queen of Hungary in June.

As a coronation gift, Hungary presented the royal couple with a country residence in Gödöllő, twenty miles east of Buda-Pest. In the next year, Elisabeth lived primarily in Gödöllő and Buda-Pest, leaving her neglected and resentful Austrian subjects to trade rumors that if the infant she was expecting were a son, she would call him Stephen (the patron saint of Hungary). The issue was avoided when she gave birth to a daughter, Marie Valerie (1868–1924). Dubbed the "Hungarian child", she was born in Buda-Pest ten months after her parents' coronation and baptised there in April. Determined to bring this last child up by herself, Elisabeth finally had her way. She poured all her repressed maternal feelings on her youngest daughter to the point of nearly smothering her. Sophie's influence over Elisabeth's children and the court faded, and she died in 1872.

Travels

Elisabeth's desk at the Achilleion in Corfu

After having achieved this victory, Elisabeth did not stay to enjoy it, but instead embarked on a life of travel, and saw little of her children. "If I arrived at a place and knew that I could never leave it again, the whole stay would become hell despite being paradise". After her son's death, at Corfu she commissioned the building of a palace which she named the *Achilleion*, after Homer's hero Achilles in *The Iliad*. After her death, the building was purchased by German Emperor Wilhelm II. Later it was acquired by the nation of Greece and converted to a museum.

Newspapers published articles on her passion for riding sports, diet and exercise regimens, and fashion sense. She often shopped at the Budapest fashion house, *Antal Alter* (now Alter és Kiss), which had become very popular with the fashion-crazed crowd. Newspapers also reported on a series of reputed lovers. Although there is no verifiable evidence of her having an affair, one of her alleged lovers was George "Bay" Middleton, a dashing Anglo-Scot. He had been named as the probable lover of Lady Henrietta Blanche Hozier and father of Clementine Ogilvy Hozier (the wife of Winston Churchill). To a degree, Elisabeth tolerated her husband Franz Joseph's affair with actress Katharina Schratt.

Mayerling incident

Photograph of the imperial hunting lodge at Mayerling, in which her son Crown Prince Rudolf committed suicide in 1889

In 1889, Elisabeth's life was shattered by the death of her only son, thirty-year-old Crown Prince Rudolf. He was found dead together with his young lover Baroness Mary Vetsera. An investigation suggested it was murder-suicide by Rudolf. The scandal was known as the Mayerling Incident, after the name of Rudolf's hunting lodge in Lower Austria, where they were found.

Elisabeth never recovered from the tragedy; she sank ever deeper into melancholy. Within one year, she had lost her mother, her father, her sister, and now her son. After Rudolf's death she dressed only in black for the rest of her life. To compound her losses, Count Gyula Andrássy died a year later, on 18 February 1890. "My last and only friend is dead," she lamented. Marie Valerie declared, "...she clung to him with true and steadfast friendship as she did perhaps, to no other person." Whether their personal relationship was an intimate one or not, her feelings for him were ones she also felt for his country, and that she knew were wholeheartedly reciprocated by the Magyars.

The Mayerling scandal increased public interest in Elisabeth, and she continued to be an icon, a sensation in her own right, wherever she went. She wore long black gowns that could be buttoned up at the bottom, and carried a white parasol made of leather in addition to a concealing fan to hide her face from the curious.

Elisabeth spent little time in Austria's capital Vienna with her husband. Their correspondence increased during their last years, however, and their relationship became a warm friendship. On her imperial steamer, *Miramar*, Empress Elisabeth travelled through the Mediterranean. Her favourite places were Cap Martin on the French Riviera, where tourism had started only in the second half of the nineteenth century; Lake Geneva in Switzerland; Bad Ischl in Austria, where the imperial couple would spend the summer; and Corfu. The Empress also visited countries not usually visited by European royals at the time: Morocco, Algeria, Malta, Turkey, and Egypt. The endless travels became an escape for the empress from her life and her misery.

Assassination

An artist's rendition of the stabbing of Elisabeth by the Italian anarchist Luigi Lucheni in Geneva, 10 September 1898

In 1898, despite warnings of possible

Purported last photograph taken of Elisabeth the day before her death at Territet, Switzerland

assassination attempts, the sixty-year-old Elisabeth traveled incognito to Geneva, Switzerland. She stayed at the Hôtel Beau-Rivage, where she had been a guest the year before.

At 1:35 p.m. on Saturday, 10 September 1898, Elisabeth and Countess Irma Sztáray de Sztára et Nagymihály, her lady in waiting, left the hotel on the shore of Lake Geneva on foot to catch the steamship *Genève* for Montreux. Since the empress did "not like processions," her servants had already been ordered to leave by train for neighboring Territet.

They were walking along the promenade when the 25-year-old Italian anarchist Luigi Lucheni approached them, attempting to peer underneath the empress's parasol. According to Sztaray, as the ship's bell announced the departure, Lucheni seemed to stumble and made a movement with his hand as if he wanted to maintain his balance. In reality, in an act of "propaganda of the deed", he had stabbed Elisabeth with a sharpened needle file that was 4 inches (100 mm) long (used to file the eyes of industrial needles) that he had inserted into a wooden handle.

A former mason, railway laborer and former valet to the Prince of Aragon, Lucheni originally planned to kill the Duc d'Orleans, but the Pretender to France's throne had left Geneva earlier for the Valais. Failing to find him, the assassin selected Elisabeth when a Geneva newspaper revealed that the elegant woman traveling under the pseudonym of "Countess of Hohenembs" was the Empress Elisabeth of Austria.

"I am an anarchist by conviction...I came to Geneva to kill a sovereign, with object of giving an example to those who suffer and those who do nothing to improve their social position; it did not matter to me who the sovereign was whom I should kill...It was not a woman I struck, but an Empress; it was a crown that I had in view."

After Lucheni struck her, the empress collapsed. A coach driver helped her to her feet and alerted the Austrian concierge of the Beau-Rivage, a man named Planner, who had been watching the empress' progress toward the *Geneve*. The two women walked roughly 100 yards (91 m) to the gangway and boarded, at which point Sztaray relaxed her hold on Elisabeth's arm. The empress then lost consciousness and collapsed next to her. Sztaray called for a doctor, but only a former nurse, a fellow passenger, was available. The boat's captain, Captain Roux, was ignorant of Elisabeth's identity and since it was very hot on deck, advised the countess to disembark and take her companion back to her hotel. Meanwhile, the boat was already sailing out of the harbor. Three men carried Elisabeth to the top deck and laid her on a bench. Sztaray opened her gown, cut Elisabeth's corset laces so she could breathe. Elisabeth revived somewhat and Sztaray asked her if she was in pain, and she replied, "No". She then asked, "What has happened?" and lost consciousness again.

Countess Sztaray noticed a small brown stain beneath the Empress' left breast. Alarmed that Elisabeth had not recovered consciousness, she informed the captain of her identity, and the boat turned back to Geneva. Elisabeth was carried back to the Hotel Beau-Rivage by six sailors on a stretcher improvised from a sail, cushions and two oars. Fanny Mayer, the wife of the hotel director, a visiting nurse, and the countess undressed Elisabeth and removed her shoes, when Sztaray noticed a few small drops of blood and a small wound. When they then removed her from the stretcher to the bed she was clearly dead; Frau Mayer believed the two audible breaths she heard the Empress take as she was brought into the room were her last. Two doctors, Dr. Golay and Dr. Mayer arrived, along with a priest, who was too late to grant her absolution. Mayer incised the artery of her left arm to ascertain death, and found no blood. She was pronounced dead at 2:10 p.m. Everyone knelt down and prayed for the repose of her soul, and Countess Sztaray closed Elisabeth's eyes and joined her hands. No matter how reluctant or resentful she was of the title, Elisabeth had been the Empress of Austria for 44 years.

When Franz Joseph received the telegram informing him of Elisabeth's death, his first fear was that she had committed suicide. It was only when a third message arrived, detailing the assassination, that he was relieved of that notion. The telegram asked permission to perform an autopsy, and answer was that whatever procedures were prescribed by Swiss Law should be adhered to.

The autopsy was performed the next day by Golay, who discovered that the weapon, which had not yet been found, had penetrated 3.33 inches (85 mm) into Elisabeth's thorax, fractured the fourth rib, pierced the lung and pericardium, and penetrated the heart from the top before coming out the base of the left ventricle. Because of the sharpness and thinness of the file the wound was very narrow and, due to pressure from Elisabeth's extremely tight corseting, the hemorrhage of blood into the pericardial sac around the heart was slowed to mere drops. Until this sac filled, the beating of her heart was not impeded, which is why Elisabeth had been able to walk from the site of the assault and up the boat's boarding ramp. Had the weapon not been removed, she would have lived a while longer, as it would have acted like a plug to stop the bleeding.

Golay photographed the wound, but turned the photograph over to the Swiss Procurator-General, who had it destroyed, on the orders of Franz Joseph, along with the autopsy instruments.

As Geneva shuttered itself in mourning, Elisabeth's body was placed in a triple coffin: two inner ones of lead, the third exterior one in bronze, reposing on lion claws. On Tuesday, before the coffins were sealed, Franz Joseph's official representatives arrived to identify the body. The coffin was fitted with two glass panels, covered with doors, which could be slid back to allow her face to be seen.

On Wednesday morning, Elisabeth's body was carried back to Vienna aboard a funeral train. The inscription on her coffin read, "Elisabeth, Empress of Austria". The Hungarians were outraged and the words, "and Queen of Hungary" were hastily added. The entire Austro-Hungarian Empire was in deep mourning; 82 sovereigns and high-ranking nobles followed her funeral cortege on the morning of 17 September to the tomb in the Church of the Capuchins. Elisabeth, who fled protocol all her life, was unable to escape it in death. Like all 15 Habsburg empresses before her, her body was buried in the crypt, but her heart was sent to the Augustinian Church, where she was married, and her internal organs were placed in the crypt of the Metropolitan Church of Saint Stephen.

Aftermath

After the attack, Lucheni fled down the Rue des Alpes, where he threw the file into the entrance to No. 3. He was caught by two cabdrivers and a sailor, then secured by a gendarme. The weapon was found the next day by the concierge during his morning cleaning; he thought it belonged to a laborer who had moved the day before and did not notify the police of his discovery until the following day. There was no blood on the file and the tip was broken off, which occurred when Lucheni threw it away. The file was so dull in appearance it was speculated that it had been

Empress Elisabeth's tomb next to that of her husband Franz Joseph in Vienna's Imperial Crypt, on the other side of Franz Josef's tomb is that of their son, Crown Prince Rudolf

deliberately selected because it would be less noticeable than a shiny knife, which would have given Lucheni away as he approached. Lucheni had planned to purchase a stiletto, but lacking the price of 12 francs he had simply sharpened an old file into a homemade dagger and cut down a piece of firewood into a handle.

Although Lucheni boasted that he acted alone, because many political refugees found a haven in Switzerland, the possibility that he was part of a plot and that the life of the emperor was also in danger, was considered. Once it was discovered that an Italian was responsible for Elisabeth's murder, unrest swept Vienna and reprisals were threatened against Italians. The intensity of shock, mourning, and outrage far exceeded that which occurred at the news of Rudolf's death. An outcry also immediately erupted over the lack of protection for the empress. The Swiss police were well aware of her presence, and telegrams to the appropriate authorities advising them to take all precautions had been dispatched. Police Chief Virieux of the Canton of Vaud had organized Elisabeth's protection, but she had detected his officers outside the hotel the day before the assassination and protested that the surveillance was disagreeable, so Virieux had no choice but to withdraw them. It is also possible that if Elisabeth had not dismissed her other attendants that day, an entourage larger than one lady-in-waiting could have discouraged Lucheni, who had been following the Empress for several days, awaiting an opportunity.

Lucheni was brought before the Geneva Court in October. Furious that the death sentence had been abolished in Geneva, he demanded that he be tried according to the laws of the Canton of Lucerne, which still had the death penalty, signing the letter: "Luigi Lucheni, anarchist, and one of the most dangerous".

Since Elisabeth was famous for preferring the common man to courtiers, known for her charitable works, and considered such a blameless target, Lucheni's sanity was questioned initially. Elisabeth's will stipulated that a large part of her jewel collection should be sold and the proceeds, then estimated at over £600,000, were to be applied to various religious and charitable organizations. Franz Joseph remarked to Prince Leichtenstein, who was the couple's devoted equerry, "That a man could be found to attack such a woman, whose whole life was spent in doing good and who never injured any person, is to me incomprehensible". Everything outside of the crown jewels and state property that Elisabeth had the power to bequeath was left to her granddaughter, the Archduchess Elisabeth, Rudolf's child.

Lucheni was declared to be sane, but was tried as a common murderer, not a political criminal. Incarcerated for life, and denied the opportunity to make a political statement by his action, he attempted to kill himself with the sharpened key from a tin of sardines on 20 February 1900. Ten years later, he hanged himself with his belt in his cell on the evening of 16 October 1910, after a guard confiscated and destroyed his uncompleted memoirs.

Legacy

Monument to Empress Elisabeth in Vienna's Volksgarten, constructed in 1907

Empress Elisabeth Western Railway commemorative coin

In 1988, historian Brigitte Hamann wrote *The Reluctant Empress*, a biography of Elisabeth, reviving interest in Franz Joseph's consort. Unlike previous portrayals of Elisabeth as a one-dimensional fairy tale princess, Hamann portrayed her as a bitter, unhappy woman full of self-loathing and various emotional and mental disorders. She was seen to have searched for happiness, but died a broken woman who never found it. Hamann's portrayal explored new facets of the legend of Sisi, as well as contemplating the role of women in high-level politics and dynasties.

Various residences that Elisabeth frequented, including her apartments in the Hofburg and the Schönbrunn Palace in Vienna, the imperial villa in Ischl, the Achilleion in Corfu, and her summer residence in Gödöllő, Hungary are preserved and open to the public.

Several sites in Hungary are named after her: two of Budapest's districts, Erzsébetváros and Pesterzsébet, and Elisabeth Bridge.

Empress Elisabeth and the Empress Elisabeth Railway (West railway) named after her were recently selected as a main motif for a high value collector coin, the Empress Elisabeth Western Railway commemorative coin.

In 1998, Gerald Blanchard stole the Koechert Diamond Pearl known as the Sisi Star, a 10-pointed star of diamonds fanning out around one enormous pearl from an exhibit commemorating the 100th anniversary of her assassination at the Schönbrunn Palace in Vienna. It was one of approximately 27 jewel-encrusted pieces designed and made by court jeweler Jakob Heinrich Köchert for her to wear in her hair, which appears in the famous portrait of her by Franz Xaver Winterhalter. The Star was recovered by Canadian Police in 2007 and eventually returned to Austria. Two versions of the famous stars were created: a second type without a pearl center, was designed by court jeweller Rozet & Fischmeister. Some stars were given to ladies of the court. One set of 27 diamond stars was kept in the Imperial family; they are seen in a photograph that shows the dowry of Rudolf's daughter, the Archduchess Elisabeth, known as "Erzsi", on the occasion of her wedding to Otto Prince Windisch-Graetz in 1902.

Portrayal of Elisabeth in the Arts

Stage

In 1932 the comic operetta *Sissi* premiered in Vienna. Composed by Fritz Kreisler, the libretto was written by Ernst and Hubert Marischka, with orchestrations by Robert Russell Bennett. Although the pet name of the empress was always spelled, "Sisi," never "Sissi," this incorrect version of her name persisted in the works about her that followed.

In 1943 Jean Cocteau wrote a play about an imagined meeting between Elisabeth and her assassin, *L'Aigle à deux têtes* (The Eagle with Two Heads). It was first staged in 1946.

In 1992, the musical *Elisabeth* premièred at the Theater an der Wien in Vienna. With libretto by Michael Kunze and music by Sylvester Levay, this is probably the darkest portrayal of the Empress' life. It portrayed Elisabeth bringing a physical manifestation of death with her to the imperial court, thus destroying the Habsburg dynasty. The leading role in the premiere was played by Dutch musical singer Pia Douwes. *Elisabeth* went on to become the most successful German-language musical of all time and has enjoyed numerous productions around the world.

Ballet

In his 1978 ballet, *Mayerling* Kenneth MacMillan portrayed Elisabeth in a *pas de deux* with her son Prince Rudolf, the principal character in the ballet.

In 1993 French ballerina Sylvie Guillem appeared in a piece entitled, *Sissi, l'impératice anarchiste* (Sissi, Anarchist Empress), choreographed by Maurice Béjart to Strauss's *Emperor Waltz*.

Film

The 1921 film *Kaiserin Elisabeth von Österreich* was one of the first films to focus entirely on Elisabeth. It was co-written by Elisabeth's niece, Marie Larisch (who played her younger self at the age of 62), and starred Carla Nelsen as the title character. The film later achieved notoriety when a group of con-artists started selling stills from the murder scene as actual photographs of the crime.

In 1936, Columbia Pictures released *The King Steps Out*, a film version of the operetta "Sissi", directed by Josef von Sternberg. It starred opera diva Grace Moore and Franchot Tone.

Jean Cocteau directed the 1948 film version of his play *The Eagle with Two Heads*. Antonioni's 1981 film *The Mystery of Oberwald* is another adaptation of the play.

In the German-speaking world, Elisabeth's name is often associated with a trilogy of romantic films about her life directed by Ernst Marischka which starred a teenage Romy Schneider:
Sissi (1955)
Sissi — die junge Kaiserin (1956) (*Sissi — The Young Empress*)

Sissi — Schicksalsjahre einer Kaiserin (1957) (Sissi — Fateful Years of an Empress)

Forever My Love is a condensed version, with the three films edited down into one feature and dubbed in English. This version was released in North America in 1962.

In early dramatizations, Elisabeth appears as peripheral to her husband and son, and so is always shown as a mature character. Schneider's characterization of Elisabeth as a young woman is the first time the "young" empress is seen on screen. The trilogy was the first to explicitly depict the romantic myth of Sisi, and ends abruptly with her determination to live a private life. Any further exploration of the topic would have been at odds with the accepted image of the loving wife, devoted mother, and benevolent empress. The three films, newly restored, are shown every Christmas on Austrian, German, Dutch, and French television. In 2007, the films were released as The Sissi Collection with English subtitles. Schneider came to loathe the role, claiming, "Sissi sticks to me like porridge (Grießbrei)." Later she appeared as a much more realistic and fascinating Elisabeth in Luchino Visconti's Ludwig, a 1972 film about Elisabeth's cousin, Ludwig II of Bavaria. A portrait of Schneider in this film was the only one, taken from her roles, which is displayed in her home.

Ava Gardner played the Empress in the 1968 film Mayerling, in which Omar Sharif starred as Crown Prince Rudolf.

The 1991 German film called Sisi/Last Minute (original Sisi und der Kaiserkuß, (Sisi and the emperor's kiss) starred French actress Vanessa Wagner as Sisi, Nils Tavernier as Emperor Franz Joseph and Sonja Kirchberger as Helene.

In the film version of Andrew Lloyd Webber's The Phantom of the Opera, the character Christine is wearing a gown inspired by the famous portrait of Elisabeth by Winterhalter.

In 2007, German comedian and director Michael Herbig released a computer-animated parody film based on Elisabeth under the title Lissi und der wilde Kaiser (lit.: "Lissi and the Wild Emperor"). It is based on his Sissi parody sketches featured in his television show Bullyparade.

Television

In 1974, Elisabeth was portrayed in the British television series Fall of Eagles. Diane Keen played the young Elisabeth and Rachel Gurney portrayed the empress at the time of Rudolf's death.

The 1992 WGBH-TV adaptation of Agatha Christie's Miss Marple mystery The Mirror Crack'd from Side to Side centers around the shooting of a fictitious film about Elisabeth. The role of the actress portraying the empress was played by Claire Bloom.

The season five finale of the Austrian detective television series Kommissar Rex (1994) revolves around a deluded woman affected by myth of the empress. The episode, appropriately, is entitled, "Sissi."

A heavily fictionalized version of Elisabeth's younger years is portrayed in a 1997 children's series, Princess Sissi.

Arielle Dombasle portrayed Elisabeth in the 2004 television film Sissi, l'impératrice rebelle, detailing the last five days of her life.

Sandra Ceccarelli portrayed an older Elisabeth in the 2006 television dramatization of the Mayerling Incident, The Crown Prince. Her son and his lover were played by Max von Thun and Vittoria Puccini.

In December 2009, Sisi, a two-part mini-series, premiered on European television, produced by a German, Austrian and Italian partnership, starring Cristiana Capotondi as Elisabeth and David Rott as Emperor Franz Joseph. While the film falls victim to the romantic mythology surrounding the unhappy marriage of Elisabeth and Franz Joseph, the political problems of the empire and the personal troubles of the main characters are dealt with in much better detail than many other dramas.

Source http://en.wikipedia.org/wiki/Empress_Elisabeth_of_Austria

Infanta Maria Josepha of Portugal

Maria José
Duchess in Bavaria

Maria Sophie of Bavaria

Spouse Karl Theodor, Duke in Bavaria
Issue
Elisabeth, Queen of the Belgians
Marie Gabrielle, Crown Princess of Bavaria
Ludwig Wilhelm, Duke in Bavaria
Full name
Maria José Joana Eulália Leopoldina Adelaide Isabel Carolina Micaela Rafaela Gabriela Francisca de Assis e de Paula Inês Sofia Joaquina Teresa Benedita Bernardina

Father Miguel I of Portugal
Mother Adelaide of Löwenstein-Wertheim-Rosenberg
Born 19 March 1857
Schloss Bronnbach
Died 11 March 1943 (aged 85)
Munich, Germany
Religion Roman Catholic

Infanta Maria José of Portugal (Maria José Joana Eulália Leopoldina Adelaide Isabel Carolina Micaela Rafaela Gabriela Francisca de Assis e de Paula Inês Sofia Joaquina Teresa Benedita Bernardina; 19 March 1857 – Munich, March 11, 1943), sometimes known in English as *Maria Josepha*, was a Portuguese infanta, later Duchess in Bavaria by marriage. She was the maternal grandmother of King Leopold III of Belgium.

Life

Maria José was the fourth child and third daughter of King Miguel I of Portugal and his wife Adelaide of Löwenstein-Wertheim-Rosenberg. Among her sisters were Maria Ana, Grand Duchess of Luxemburg and Maria Antónia, Duchess of Parma. Her only brother was Miguel II, Duke of Braganza.

She married on April 29, 1874, Karl-Theodor, Duke in Bavaria, the younger brother of Elisabeth of Bavaria, better known as "Sissi".

The couple lived in München, where they founded the **Herzog Carl Theodor Eye Clinic**, that still exists today.

Maria José died in 1943 at the age of 85, and is buried in Tegernsee Abbey.

Children

Sophie Adelheid (1875–1957)
Elisabeth Gabriele Valérie Marie (1876–1965), future Queen Elisabeth of Belgium, married Albert I of Belgium.
Marie Gabrielle (1878–1912), married Rupprecht, Crown Prince of Bavaria.
Ludwig Wilhelm (1884–1968)
Franz Joseph (1888–1912)
Source http://en.wikipedia.org/wiki/Infanta_Maria_Josepha_of_Portugal

Maria Sophie of Bavaria

Maria Sophie of Bavaria
Queen consort of the Two Sicilies

Maria Sophie photographed by Franz Hanfstängl in 1859.
Spouse Francis II
Issue
Princess Maria Cristina Pia
House House of Wittelsbach
House of Bourbon-Two Sicilies
Father Maximilian Joseph, Duke in Bavaria
Mother Princess Ludovika of Bavaria
Born 4 October 1841
Possenhofen Castle, Possenhofen, Kingdom of Bavaria
Died 19 January 1925 (aged 83)
Munich, Bavaria, Weimar Republic
Burial Basilica of Santa Chiara, Naples
Religion Roman Catholic

Maria Sophie of Bavaria, (4 October 1841, Possenhofen Castle – 19 January 1925, Munich) was the last Queen consort of the Kingdom of the Two Sicilies. She was one of the ten children of Maximilian Joseph, Duke in Bavaria and Princess Ludovika of Bavaria. She was born as Duchess Maria Sophia in Bavaria. She was the younger sister of the better-known Elisabeth of Bavaria ("Sisi") who married Emperor Franz Joseph I of Austria.

Early life, betrothal and marriage

In the winter of 1857, at the age of 16, Marie's hand was sought by Francis II, Crown Prince of Naples, Duke of Calabria, and the eldest son of Ferdinand II of the Two Sicilies, King of Naples. The marriage was political, since Fedinand wished to ally himself with the Emperor of Austria, Franz Josef I, a powerful fellow absolutist. At that time the kingdom was already threatened by revolutionary forces. At that time Marie had not experienced menarche, and underwent treatments to try and induce menses (Hamann 80). She also had to try and learn Italian. She was married by proxy. In January 1859 she traveled to Vienna to spend time with her sister before they went to Trieste to formally enter her new kingdom, and say farewell to her family on the Neapolitan royal yacht *Fulminante*. She set sail for Bari and 3 February 1859 was married there. (Hamann 82).

Queen

Francis turned out to be mentally and physically ill, a religious fanatic and impotent (Hamann 84). Within the year, with the death of the king, her husband ascended to the throne as Francis II of the Two Sicilies, and Maria Sophie became queen of a realm that was shortly to be overwhelmed by the forces of Giuseppe Garibaldi and Piedmontese army.

In September 1860, as the Garibaldine troops were moving towards Naples, his capital, Francis II decided to leave the city. At the beginning, he planned to organise a resistance in Capua. However, after that city had also been lost to the Garibaldines in the aftermath of the battle of the Volturnus (October), he and Marie Sophie took refuge in the strong coastal fortress of Gaeta, 80 km north of Naples.

During the Siege of Gaeta in late 1860 and early 1861, the forces of Victor Emmanuel II bombarded and eventually overcame the defenders. It was this brief "last stand of the Bourbons" that gained Maria Sophia the reputation of the strong "warrior queen" and "heroine of Gaeta" (Hamann1986, p 129) that stayed with her for the rest of her life. She was tireless in her efforts to rally the defenders, giving them her own food, caring for the wounded, and daring the attackers to come within range of the fortress cannon.

Rome

With the fall of Gaeta and the Kingdom of the Two Sicilies, Maria Sophia and her husband went into exile in Rome, the capital of what for 1,000 years had been the sizeable Papal States, a large piece of central Italy but which, by 1860, had been reduced to the city of Rome, itself, as the armies of Victor Emanuel II came down from the north to join up with Garibaldi, the conqueror of the south. King Francis set up a government in exile in Rome that enjoyed diplomatic recognition by most European states for a few years as still the legitimate government of the Kingdom of the Two Sicilies.

Her wealth and privilege were, to a certain extent, overshadowed by personal tragedies. Her marriage was not consummated for many years, as her husband suffered from phimosis. His shyness and religious fanaticism also prevented the couple from developing any kind of physical intimacy with each other. While in exile in Rome, Maria fell in love with an officer of the papal guard, Armand de Lawayss, and became pregnant by him. She retreated to her parents' home at Possenhofen, where a family council decided that she must give birth in secret to prevent scandal. On 24 November 1862, Maria Sophie gave birth to a daughter in St. Ursula's Convent in Augsburg. The child was immediately given to Lawayss' family. Maria Sophia was made to promise that she would never see her again, which deeply affected her. Maria Sophie suffered from depression in later life, which is believed to have been rooted in this event.

A year later, on the advice of her family, Maria Sophia decided to confess the affair to her husband. Afterwards, the relationship between the two improved for a time. Francis submitted to an operation which allowed him to consummate the marriage, and Maria became pregnant a second time, this time by her husband. Both were overjoyed at the turn of events and full of hope. On 24 December 1869, after ten years of marriage, Marie Sophie gave birth to a daughter, Maria Cristina Pia. Cristina was born on the birthday of her aunt, Empress Elisabeth, who became her godmother. Unfortunately, the baby lived only three months and died on 28 March 1870. Maria Sophie and her husband never had another child.

Later life

In 1870, Rome fell to the forces of Italy and the King and Queen fled to Bavaria. The king died in 1894. Maria Sophia spent time in Munich, and then moved to Paris where she presided over somewhat of an informal Bourbon court-in-exile. It was rumored she was involved in the anarchist assassination of King Humbert in 1900 in hopes of destabilizing the new nation-state of Italy. Recent historians have resurrected that rumor based on the apparent credence given to this conspiracy theory by the then Prime Minister of Italy, Giovanni Giolitti. Others regard it as anecdotal. In any event, the case against Maria Sophia is circumstantial.

During World War I, Maria Sophie was actively on the side of the German Empire and Austria-Hungary in their war with the Kingdom of Italy. Again, the rumors claimed she was involved in sabotage and espionage against Italy in the hope that an Italian defeat would tear the nation apart and that the kingdom of Naples would be restored.

During her life, she generated an almost cult-like air of admiration even among her political enemies. Gabriele D'Annunzio called her the "stern little Bavarian eagle" and Marcel Proust spoke of the "soldier queen on the ramparts of Gaeta". She and her sister Elisabeth were considered amongst the great beauties of their age. (Hamann 1986, p 129)

Maria Sophie died in Munich in 1925. From 1984 her remains now rest with those of her husband and their daughter in the Church of Santa Chiara in Naples.

Titles and styles

4 October 1841 – 3 February 1859 *Her Royal Highness* Duchess Maria Sophie in Bavaria
3 February 1859 – 22 May 1859 *Her Royal Highness* the Duchess of Calabria
22 May 1859 – 27 December 1894 *Her Majesty* the Queen of the Two Sicilies
27 December 1894 – 19 January 1925 *Her Majesty* the Dowager Queen of the Two Sicilies

Genealogy

Ancestors

Siblings

Marie of Baden-Sponheim

Notes and citations

This item originated as an abridged and edited version of an article that appears in an online encyclopedia of Naples and has been inserted here by the author and copyright holder of that article.

Marie of Baden-Sponheim

Marie of Baden-Sponheim

Maria Jacobäa von Baden, wife of Duke Wilhelm IV of Bavaria (Hans Schöpfer I)

Spouse(s)	William IV, Duke of Bavaria
Noble family	House of Zähringen
Father	Philip I, Margrave of Baden
Mother	Elisabeth of the Palatinate
Born	25 June 1507
Died	16 November 1580 (aged 73) Munich

Marie Jakobaea of Baden-Sponheim (25 June 1507 – 16 November 1580, Munich) was a German noblewoman and (by marriage) duchess of Bavaria.

Life

Marie was the daughter of Philip I, Margrave of Baden (1479–1533) and Countess Elisabeth (1483–1522), daughter of Philip, Elector Palatine and princess Margarete von Bayern-Landshut. Her paternal grandparents were Christopher I, Margrave of Baden-Baden and Ottilie of Katzenelnbogen.

On 5 October 1522 she married William IV, Duke of Bavaria (1493–1550), eldest son of Albert IV and his wife Kunigunde of Austria. They had four children:
Theodo (1526–1534)
Albert V (1528–1579) ∞ 1546 Archduchess Anna of Austria (1528–1590)
Wilhelm (1529–1530)
Mechthild of Bavaria (1532–1565) ∞ 1557 Margrave Philibert of Baden-Baden (1536–1569)

Source http://en.wikipedia.org/wiki/Marie_of_Baden-Sponheim

Princess Amalie of Saxe-Coburg and Gotha

Princess Amalie of Saxe-Coburg and Gotha

Duchess Amalie in Bavaria

Spouse	Duke Maximilian Emanuel in Bavaria

Issue
Duke Siegfried
Duke Christoph
Duke Luitpold

Full name
German: *Marie Luise Franziska Amalie*

House	House of Saxe-Coburg and Gotha House of Wittelsbach
Father	Prince August of Saxe-Coburg and Gotha
Mother	Princess Clémentine of Orléans
Born	23 October 1848 Coburg, Saxe-Coburg and Gotha
Died	6 May 1894 (aged 45) Schloss Biederstein, Schwabing, Munich, Kingdom of Bavaria

Princess Marie Luise Franziska Amalie of Saxe-Coburg and Gotha, full German name: *Marie Luise Franziska Amalie, Prinzessin von Sachsen-Coburg und Gotha, Herzogin zu Sachsen* (23 October 1848, Coburg, Saxe-Coburg and Gotha – 6 May 1894, Schloss Biederstein, Schwabing, Munich, Kingdom of Bavaria) was a Princess of Saxe-Coburg and Gotha by birth and a Duchess in Bavaria through her marriage to Duke Maximilian Emanuel in Bavaria. Amalie was the fourth child and second eldest daughter of Prince August of Saxe-Coburg and Gotha and his wife Princess Clémentine of Orléans. Her youngest brother was Ferdinand I of Bulgaria.

Marriage and issue

From childhood, Amalie had been intended as the bride of Prince Leopold of Bavaria. However, Duke Maximilian Emanuel in Bavaria, youngest child of Duke Maximilian Joseph in Bavaria and his wife Princess Ludovika of Bavaria, fell in love with her and confided this love in his sister Elisabeth of Bavaria, now Empress of Austria.

The Empress became determined to ensure her favorite brother's happiness. She invited Leopold for an extended visit with the imperial family, among whom was her own fifteen-year-old daughter Archduchess Gisela of Austria. There, Leopold was tactfully made aware that a marriage with Gisela would be looked upon with favor by Emperor Franz Joseph. The temptation to become the Emperor's son-in-law was too strong to resist, and Leopold became engaged to Gisela after only a few days. After a sufficient amount of time had passed to enable Amalie to recover, Empress Elisabeth brought Max and Amalie together. They were married on 20 September 1875 in Ebenthal, Lower Austria, Austria–Hungary.

Amalie and Maximilian Emanuel had three sons:
Siegfried August Maximilian Maria, Duke in Bavaria (10 July 1876–12 March 1952)
Christoph Joseph Clemens Maria, Duke in Bavaria (22 April 1879–10 July 1963)
Luitpold Emanuel Ludwig Maria, Duke in Bavaria (30 June 1890–16 January 1973)
The marriage was by all accounts a very happy one.

Titles, styles, honours and arms

Titles and styles

23 October 1848 – 20 September 1875: *Her Serene Highness* Princess Amalie of Saxe-Coburg and Gotha, Duchess of Saxony
20 September 1875 – 6 May 1894: *Her Royal Highness* Duchess Amalie in Bavaria, Princess of Saxe-Coburg and Gotha, Duchess of Saxony

Ancestry

Source http://en.wikipedia.org/wiki/Princess_Amalie_of_Saxe-Coburg_and_Gotha

Princess Amélie Louise of Arenberg

Princess Amélie Louise of Arenberg
Duchess Amélie Louise in Bavaria

Spouse	Duke Pius August in Bavaria
Issue	
	Duke Maximilian Joseph
Full name	
	French: *Amélie Louise*
House	House of Arenberg House of Wittelsbach
Father	Duke Louis Marie of Arenberg
Mother	Marie Adélaïde Julie de Mailly, dame d'Ivry-sur-Seine
Born	10 April 1789 Brussels, Austrian Netherlands
Died	4 April 1823 (aged 33) Bamberg, Kingdom of Bavaria
Burial	Tegernsee Abbey

Princess and Duchess Amélie Louise of Arenberg, full German name: *Amalie Luise, Prinzessin und Herzogin von Arenberg* and full French name: *Amélie Louise, princesse et duchesse d'Arenberg*, (born 10 April 1789 in Brussels, Austrian Netherlands; died 4 April 1823 in Bamberg, Kingdom of Bavaria) was a member of the House of Arenberg by birth and, through her marriage to Duke Pius August in Bavaria, a member of the Palatinate-Birkenfeld-Gelnhausen line of the House of Wittelsbach. Amélie Louise was a grandmother of Empress Elisabeth of Austria through her son Duke Maximilian Joseph in Bavaria.

Early life

Born in Brussels, Austrian Netherlands, Amélie Louise was the daughter of Prince Louis Marie d'Arenberg and his first wife, Marie Adélaïde Julie de Mailly, dame d'Ivry-sur-Seine.

Marriage and issue

Amélie Louise married Duke Pius August in Bavaria, son of Duke Wilhelm in Bavaria and his wife Countess Palatine Maria Anna of Zweibrücken-Birkenfeld, on 26 May 1807 in Brussels. Pius August and Amélie Louise had one son: Duke Maximilian Joseph in Bavaria (4 December 1808 – 15 November 1888)

After their marriage, the couple moved to Bamberg and received their son Maximilian Joseph the following year. In 1817, Amélie Louise sent her only son to reside with his great uncle Maximilian I Joseph of Bavaria, where he studied at the Royal Institute of Education. Amélic Louise did not see him until 1820. Shortly after returning from her second visit to Munich, Amélie Louise died in 1823 in Bamberg. She was interred in the burial crypt of Tegernsee Abbey.

Titles, styles, honours and arms

Titles and styles

10 April 1789 – 26 May 1807: *Her Serene Highness* Princess and Duchess Amélie Louise of Arenberg
26 May 1807 – 4 April 1823: *Her Royal Highness* Duchess Amélie Louise in Bavaria

Ancestry

Source http://en.wikipedia.org/wiki/Princess_Amélie_Louise_of_Arenberg

Princess Ludovika of Bavaria

Marie Ludovika Wilhelmine, Prince

Princess Sophie of Saxony

Spouse	Maximilian Joseph, Duke in
Issue	
Ludwig Wilhelm, Duke in Bavaria	
Wilhelm Karl, Duke in Bavaria	
Helene, Hereditary Princess of Thurn	
Elisabeth, Empress of Austria	
Karl Theodor, Duke in Bavaria	
Marie Sophie, Queen of the Two Sicili	
Mathilde Ludovika, Countess of Trani	
Maximilian, Duke in Bavaria	
Sophie Charlotte, Duchess of Alençon	
Duke Maximilian Emanuel in Bavaria	
House	House of Wittelsbach
Father	Maximilian I Joseph of Bav
Mother	Karoline of Baden
Born	30 August 1808 Munich, Kingdom of E
Died	25 January 1892 (aged 83) Munich, Germany

Princess Ludovika of Bavaria (Marie helmine; English: Mary Louise Wilhelm 1808 – 25 January 1892) was the sixth Maximilian I Joseph of Bavaria and his Karoline of Baden. She was born and d

Biography

Marriage

Ludovika married Maximilian Joseph, (December 4, 1808 - November 15, 18 Duke Pius August in Bavaria was her c tember 9, 1828, in Tegernsee. They ha

Children

Name	Birth	Death	
Ludwig Wilhelm, Duke in Bavaria ("Louis")	21 June 1831	6 November 1920 (aged 89)	
Wilhelm Karl, Duke in Bavaria	24 December 1832	13 February 1833 (aged 0)	
Helene Caroline Therese, Duchess in Bavaria ("Néné")	4 April 1834	16 May 1890 (aged 56)	
Elisabeth Amalie Eugenie, Duchess in Bavaria (Sisi)	24 December 1837	10 September 1898 (aged 60)	
Karl Theodor "Gackl"	9 August 1839	30 November 1909 (aged 70)	
Marie Sophie Amalie, Duchess in Bavaria	4 October 1841	19 January 1925 (aged 83)	
Mathilde Ludovika, Duchess in Bavaria	30 September 1843	18 June 1925 (aged 81)	
Maximilian, Duke in Bavaria	8 December 1845	8 December 1845 (aged 0)	
Sophie Charlotte Augustine, Duchess in Bavaria	23 February 1847	4 May 1897 (aged 50)	
Duke Maximilian Emanuel in Bavaria "Mapperl"	7 December 1849	12 June 1893 (aged 43)	

Ancestry

Source http://en.wikipedia.org/wiki/Pri _of_Bavaria

Princess Sophie of Saxony

Princess Sophie of Saxony
Duchess Sophie in Bavaria

Spouse	Duke Karl-Theodor in Bavaria
Issue	Amalie, Duchess of Urach
Full name	
German: *Sophie Maria Friederike Auguste Leopoldine Alexandrine Ernestine Albertine Elisabeth*	
House	House of Wettin
	House of Wittelsbach
Father	John of Saxony
Mother	Amalie Auguste of Bavaria
Born	15 March 1845
	Dresden, Kingdom of Saxony
Died	9 March 1867 (aged 21)
	Munich, Kingdom of Bavaria
Burial	Tegernsee Abbey
Religion	Roman Catholicism

Princess *Sophie* Maria Friederike Auguste Leopoldine Alexandrine Ernestine Albertine Elisabeth of Saxony, Duchess of Saxony (Full German name: *Prinzessin Sophie Maria Friederike Auguste Leopoldine Alexandrine Ernestine Albertine Elisabeth von Sachsen, Herzogin zu Sachsen*) (15 March 1845, Dresden, Kingdom of Saxony – 9 March 1867, Munich, Kingdom of Bavaria) was the eighth and youngest child of John of Saxony and his wife Amalie Auguste of Bavaria and a younger sister of Albert of Saxony and George of Saxony. Through her marriage to Duke Karl-Theodor in Bavaria, Sophie was a member of the House of Wittelsbach and a Duchess in Bavaria.

Marriage and Issue

Sophie married Duke Karl-Theodor in Bavaria, fifth child and third-eldest son of Duke Maximilian Joseph in Bavaria and his wife Princess Ludovika of Bavaria, on 11 February 1865 in Dresden. Sophie and Karl-Theodor had one child:

Duchess Amalie in Bavaria (24 December 1865 – 26 May 1912)

Illness and death

Childbirth caused severe respiratory problems for Sophie, which progressively weakened her. She managed to recover, however, a year later she contracted a severe case of influenza that she could not overcome. Sophie died shortly before her 22nd birthday on 9 March 1867 and was interred at Tegernsee Abbey.

Titles, styles, honours and arms

Titles and styles

15 March 1845 – 11 February 1865: *Her Royal Highness* Princess Sophie of Saxony, Duchess of Saxony

11 February 1865 – 9 March 1867: *Her Royal Highness* Duchess Sophie in Bavaria, Princess and Duchess of Saxony

Ancestry

Source http://en.wikipedia.org/wiki/Princess_Sophie_of_Saxony

Sophie, Hereditary Princess of Liechtenstein

Duchess Sophie in Bavaria	
Hereditary Princess of Liechtenstein	
Spouse	Alois, Hereditary Prince of Liechtenstein
Issue	
Prince Joseph Wenzel	
Princess Marie Caroline	
Prince Georg Antonius	
Prince Nikolaus Sebastian	
Full name	
Sophie Elisabeth Marie Gabrielle	
House	House of Wittelsbach
	House of Liechtenstein
Father	Prince Max, Duke in Bavaria
Mother	Countess Elisabeth Douglas
Born	28 October 1967
	Munich, Germany

Sophie, Hereditary Princess of Liechtenstein (German: *Sophie, Erbprinzessin von und zu Liechtenstein*, née *Duchess Sophie in Bavaria, Princess of Bavaria*; born 28 October 1967 in Munich), is the wife of Alois, Hereditary Prince of Liechtenstein, Regent of Liechtenstein and heir apparent to the Liechtensteiner throne.

Early life and education

Hereditary Princess Sophie was born in Munich on 28 October 1967 as the eldest of the five daughters of Prince Max, Duke in Bavaria, and Swedish Countess Elisabeth Douglas. Through her father, she is a direct descendant of the last King of Bavaria, Ludwig III (1845-1921), who was her great-great-grandfather.

Sophie spent her childhood together with her parents and sisters in Wildbad Kreuth. From 1978 to 1980, Sophie attended the Girls' Home Primary School of the English Lady in Heiligenstadt. She then moved to the Girls' Secondary Boarding School Hohenburg in Lenggries. Sophie then studied English language and literature at the Catholic University in Eichstätt.

Marriage and children

Sophie married Hereditary Prince Alois of Liechtenstein on 3 July 1993 at St. Florin's in Vaduz, Liechtenstein. They

have four children:
Prince Joseph Wenzel Maximilian Maria of Liechtenstein (born 24 May 1995 in London)
Princess Marie-Caroline Elisabeth Immaculata of Liechtenstein (born 17 October 1996 in Grabs, Canton of St. Gallen)
Prince Georg Antonius Constantin Maria of Liechtenstein (born 20 April 1999 in Grabs)
Prince Nikolaus Sebastian Alexander Maria of Liechtenstein, Count of Rietberg (born 6 December 2000, in Grabs)

Bavarian Royal Family

HRH The Duke of Bavaria
HRH The Duke in Bavaria
HRH The Duchess in Bavaria
HRH The Hereditary Princess of Liechtenstein
HRH Marie-Caroline, Duchess Philipp of Württemberg
HRH Princess Hélène
HRH Princess Elisabeth, Mrs. Daniel Terberger
HRH Princess Maria Anna, Mrs. Klaus Runow
HRH The Princess of Waldburg-Zeil
HRH The Princess of Quadt

Failing the birth of a male heir, which seems unlikely, the Jacobite claim to the thrones of England, Scotland, Ireland and France will pass to Sophie, following the demise of the current holder, her childless uncle Franz, Duke of Bavaria, and of her own father, who has no sons. However, Sophie is not in the line of the Bavarian succession, as Semi-Salic law prevents a female from becoming head of the House of Wittelsbach, so long as any male member of the dynasty, howsoever distantly related to the current head, survives.

Titles, styles, honours and arms

Styles of
Sophie, Hereditary Princess of Liechtenstein

Reference style Her Royal Highness
Spoken style Your Royal Highness
Alternative style Ma'am

Titles and styles

28 October 1967 - 1973: *Her Royal Highness* Princess Sophie of Bavaria
1973 - 3 July 1993: *Her Royal Highness* Duchess Sophie in Bavaria, Princess of Bavaria
3 July 1993 – present: *Her Royal Highness* The Hereditary Princess of Liechtenstein, Countess of Rietberg

From her birth Sophie was styled **Princess Sophie of Bavaria**. In 1973, her father inherited the family name and style Duke in Bavaria from his great-uncle who had adopted him as heir in 1965; Sophie was then styled **Duchess Sophie in Bavaria, Princess of Bavaria**. On her marriage in 1993 she became **HRH The Hereditary Princess of Liechtenstein, Countess of Rietberg**, the Principality of Liechtenstein recognising and retaining her use of the style *Royal Highness*.

Ancestry

Source http://en.wikipedia.org/wiki/Sophie,_Hereditary_Princess_of_Liechtenstein